Indian Legacy

Native American Influences on World Life and Culture

Indian Legacy

Native American Influences on World Life and Culture

Hermina Poatgieter

ILLUSTRATED

JULIAN MESSNER   NEW YORK   SIP

/5877

JULIAN MESSNER and colophon are trademarks of
Simon & Schuster, registered in the U.S. Patent
and Trademark Office.

Manufactured in the United States of America.
Design by Irving Perkins Associates.

Library of Congress Cataloging in Publication Data

Poatgieter, Alice Hermina.
    Indian legacy.

    Bibliography: p.
    Includes index.
    Summary: Discusses the many important contri-
butions made by the Indians of North and South
America to civilization throughout the world.
    1. Indians—Juvenile literature. 2. Civiliza-
tion—Indian influences—Juvenile literature.
3. United States—Civilization—Indian influences
—Juvenile literature. [1. Civilization—Indian
influences. 2. Indians] I. Title.
E59.I53P63   970.004'97   81-14171

ISBN 0-671-41703-7   AACR2

*To the American Indian children, who should know the
great gifts that their people have given the world.*

Acknowledgments

I WISH to acknowledge my gratitude to Professor Virgil J. Vogel, Truman College, Chicago, who read the entire manuscript and gave me excellent critical advice; to Dr. Frederick J. Dockstader, former director of the Museum of the American Indian, Heye Foundation, who read and criticized the chapter on art; to Professor George Sprague, University of Illinois, who read and criticized the chapter on corn; and to Dr. Louis B. Casagrande, curator of anthropology, Science Museum of Minnesota, who advised me on matters which concerned anthropology in the manuscript. The maps were drawn by cartographer Lisa D. Fryxell.

The quotation of Peter Farb is from *Man's Rise to Civilization as Shown by the Indians of North America from Primeval Times to the Coming of the Industrial State* by Peter Farb. Copyright © 1968, Peter Farb. Published by E. P. Dutton, Inc., New York.

The quotation of Felix Cohen is from "Americanizing the White Man" by Felix S. Cohen. *The American Scholar*, Spring 1957. Copyright, Felix S. Cohen.

The quotation of John Collier is from *The Indians of the Americas* by John Collier. Published by W. W. Norton and Co., New York, 1947. Copyright, The New American Library.

The quotation of George Beadle is from "The Ancestry of Corn" by George Beadle. *Scientific American*, January 1980.

Contents

Introduction

OUR AMERICAN way of life has its roots in all parts of the globe. Peoples from every region have made their contributions. Few of us, however, realize what a very large part of our way of life has come from the Indians, the first inhabitants of North and South America. Our American heritage is in large part Indian.

Because the two hemispheres of the earth are separated from each other by the Atlantic Ocean on one side and the Pacific on the other, civilization developed separately in the two parts in ancient times, neither half knowing about the other. On the continents of the Eastern Hemisphere—Europe, Asia, Africa, Australia—primitive tribes began to grow crops, domesticate animals, govern themselves, and in some places to found great civilizations. Meanwhile, in the Western Hemisphere, on the two continents later to be called the Americas, lived peoples who did the same. In the course of thousands of years these first Americans, now known as Indians, created many cultures, some of them highly advanced.

A few people would still like to believe that the cultures of the Indians were brought from the Eastern Hemisphere by now-forgotten immigrants. It is hardly possible that this happened. Certainly men and women from the other side of the world came to the Americas before Christopher Columbus, but they did not stay. The records are dim and uncertain, and the visitors left no evidence of their way of life—such as horses, wheat, sheep, or iron plows.

Finally, however, a firm and lasting contact was made between the two hemispheres. When Columbus, in 1492, sailed west from Spain in search of a safer, shorter route to the Orient, he came to a place he felt sure was Asia (then known as the Indies) and called the people he saw there Indians. Some time passed before Europeans realized that the place Columbus had reached was not Asia, but a strange land that the Eastern Hemisphere had never heard of.

Columbus did not come to an empty land, but to one rich in a variety of ancient cultures and peoples. The main civilizations in the Americas at the time he arrived were those of the Incas of Peru and the Aztecs in Mexico. The peak of the Maya civilization had passed, and the Mound Builders of the Mississippi Valley had disappeared. Some well-developed life-styles, however, flourished among the peoples north of Mexico. These were encountered by explorers who came after Columbus.

As soon as the first European ships touched the shores of the Americas, cultural exchange began between the two hemispheres. On his first voyage, Columbus carried back strange birds, plants, animals, and "other things never seen or heard tell of in Spain." He left with the Indians objects from Europe that were new to them. The Indians took an active part in this cultural exchange.

The Europeans who followed Columbus also at once came under the influence of Indian ways: the Spanish who invaded and conquered Mexico and Peru in the 1500s and the English and French who explored and colonized the Atlantic coast of North America in the 1600s. Indian influence has made itself felt without interruption ever since. Today life in the United States—in fact, life on earth—is far different from what it would have been if Columbus had found no one living in the two Americas.

Centuries passed before anyone began to realize what a tremendous contribution the Indian people have made to human welfare and progress. Not until four hundred years after Columbus's first voyage did a few scholars begin to look at the records and see that ideas and objects from the first Americans have affected life in all nations indeed, that the American Indians are major contributors to world culture. In this respect, as anthropologist Peter Farb put it, "the Indian appears to have won out over his White conqueror." Even today, this is largely unknown and unappreciated. Daniel Boorstin, librarian of Congress, calls it a "neglected subject."

The influence of the Indians on our own country is especially great. Their effect on ideas that were brought to America by Europeans produced a new way of life. The first Americans helped determine much of our history and shape the political ideas of the nation. Their effect on agriculture alone can be shown by one example: nearly half the total value of our farm crops comes from plants that were developed from wild growths, through centuries of plant breeding, by Indian agriculturalists. This is not a tradition or a legend, but a traceable, historical fact. Records show that contributions from the first Americans are an important part of our national arts, diet, customs, language, medical science, sports, government, industries, clothing, agriculture, and almost every other phase of life.

Part I

1

Indian Influence on Government and Political Ideas in the United States

ALTHOUGH MATERIAL wealth from Indian cultures has enriched many nations of the world, Native American "gifts of the spirit" have also had a profound effect on other peoples. These Indian attitudes and values, different from many that the Europeans brought to the New World, have had a special influence on the United States. They have changed the course of events at important points in history and have given life here much of its special character. Many of our most prized traditions, which people call typically American, can be linked to ideas the Indian people held. The scholar Felix S. Cohen said, "What is distinctive about America is Indian through and through." These influences are not so easy to trace as the material benefits, but the records tell us much.

All the first Europeans in the Americas had dealings with Indian people. When they arrived, the Indians gave them food, guided them through forests and across mountains, and taught them how to survive in the New World. Throughout the 1600s and 1700s the English colonists along the Atlantic had constant dealings with the Native Americans.

They carried on extensive fur trade with Indians, conferred with them about land settlements and peace agreements, and made alliances with them against common white or Indian enemies. In these situations the Europeans learned something of the ideals and principles of the Indian people—what they valued, how they solved life's problems. Here the immigrants came up against a number of ideas that sharply challenged their European ways of thinking.

One such idea was that of forming a union. Although the colonies along the Atlantic had many things in common, they were not friendly with one another. Some were rivals for Indian trade; some tried to cheat one another over boundaries; most did not tolerate one another's religious beliefs. Yet in dealing with common problems they could have gained advantages if they had forgotten their differences and acted together. Here the Iroquois League set them a great example. This league, founded in 1570, was a permanent union of five, later six, Indian nations. It lasted for centuries. Its purpose was to establish peace among the peoples through a government based on justice and equality. The aim of the founders was to include more and more nations "until all tribes of men were united in everlasting peace and brotherhood." The colonists were much impressed with this organization. The league was a confederation—that is, a union of self-governing states or nations in which each member gave up power to the central government in those matters they all shared. Its constitution had features that were rare in any government at the time.

At one of the councils in which colonial governors met with representatives of the league, in the mid-1700s, the Iroquois leader Canasatego (kah nah sah TAY go) advised the colonists to form a union like theirs: "Our wise forefathers established Union and Amity between the five Nations. This has made us formidable; this has given us great Weight and Authority with our neighboring Nations. We are a powerful Confederacy; and by your observing the same methods that our Wise Forefathers have taken, you will acquire such Strength and Power."

The colonial statesman Benjamin Franklin saw this as good advice and freely acknowledged his debt to the Indian teachers: "It would be strange," he advised a later council, "if Six Nations of [Indians] should be capable of forming a scheme for such a union and be able to execute it in such a manner that it has subsisted for ages, and appears indissoluble, and yet that a like union should be impracticable for ten or a dozen English colonies, to whom it is more necessary and must be more advantageous, and who cannot be supposed to lack an equal understanding of their interest." Franklin drew up such a plan of union for the colonies in 1754, modeled after the Iroquois example, but it was not accepted. The colonies were not yet ready to see that they could benefit from such a step.

The colonies, especially the northern ones, desperately needed to be strengthened by union, because of threats from the French and their Indian allies in Canada. The French had entered the St. Lawrence Valley in the early 1600s when the Dutch and British were settling along the Atlantic seaboard. In Canada the French established Montreal, Quebec, and other settlements and organized a fur trade reaching westward through the Great Lakes and southward along the Mississippi. Before the end of the 1600s they began to push their control into Indian lands also being claimed by the English. The result was a series of conflicts between England and France on North American soil known as the French and Indian Wars, lasting from 1689 to 1763. In this struggle, the Iroquois decided the outcome. The French allied themselves with the Algonquins in Canada. The English colonies were able to get help from the mighty Iroquois League, the core of which was located in central New York.

The colonists, who were few and weak, went to great lengths to get and keep the friendship of the league, which they needed for defense. It was the Iroquois who kept the

French and their Indian allies from coming down from Canada and wiping out the northern settlements. In the 1760s, with Iroquois help, the English were finally victorious, and the French lost their claims in eastern Canada and east of the Mississippi. The Iroquois alliance with the British was one of the most significant factors in the first 150 years of colonial history. Historians generally agree that it was Iroquois power that tipped the balance and enabled the English, not the French, finally to dominate the American continent north of Mexico.

When the thirteen original states drew up their Articles of Confederation, their first supreme law, Iroquois influence was again felt, for the articles were patterned after Franklin's plan of union, which had used the Iroquois League as a model. When Franklin spoke of the league, he said that the Iroquois had "formed a scheme for such a union," that is, a certain kind of union, and he believed the English colonies could form "a like union," that is, one like the league. The colonists were well acquainted with Iroquois government, because when they met with Indian statesmen to discuss trade or diplomatic matters, they did so under the league's rules. They understood how the league formed a balance between its central government and the powers reserved by the various states that made up the league. When the United States Constitution replaced the Articles of Confederation, its framers had to solve this problem when they wrote the laws governing a union of independent states. In some important respects, they followed the plan of the successful, long-standing Iroquois League.

Like the Iroquois, most other Indian peoples living north of Mexico held democratic attitudes and beliefs that were not common among English colonists. In their long association with the Native Americans, the colonists and, later, the settlers found many groups in which members respected one another's rights, considered themselves free and equal, and each had a voice in decisions made for the group. The

English colonists found that many Indians believed that government should control people as little as possible, that it can exist only with the people's consent, and that they have the power to change it. These ideas were reported by explorers, traders, settlers, and many others, who clearly considered them unusual.

Of the Huron people a man wrote in the 1600s, "They are a free people, each of whom considers himself of as much consequence as the others, and they submit to their chiefs only in so far as it pleases them." An account written in 1700 says of the Illinois Indians, "All men seem equal to them. An Illini would speak as boldly to the King of France as to the lowest of his subjects." A man in the Ohio Valley wrote during the same period, "Amongst the Indians all people are equal, personal qualities being most esteemed." Citizens of the Iroquois League, wrote another, had "such absolute notions of liberty that they allow no kind of superiority of one over another." Later, Indian writers described their cultures in the same terms. In the Iroquois League all people could vote: men, women, and children—children's votes being cast by their mothers. In the various colonies, only white men could vote, or in some places only those men who owned property or who belonged to a certain church. True, life on the frontier helped to level any social classes that were brought from Europe, but democracy as practiced among American Indians was not found among the men and women who owed allegiance to a king.

Many people today are fond of saying, "This is a free country." For the Indian people we are speaking of, it really was a free land. Of the Illinois tribe, the man quoted above continued, "They live in peace, which is due in great measure to the fact that each one is allowed to do as he pleases." The explorer Meriwether Lewis wrote of the Indian people he met in his journey to the Pacific with William Clark that the nature of their government was "perfectly free from restraint." A settler in the Ohio Valley in the 1700s wrote that

Indians in Council by Seth Eastman, painted in 1850, shows a meeting of Dakota (also called Sioux) leaders. The first Europeans in North America found that most Indian nations north of Mexico were intensely

democratic. When the need arose, the affairs of the people were guided by councils, but the leaders were looked on as public servants, not as rulers.

the love of liberty is inborn in the Indian and "seems to be the ruling passion of his nature." Jefferson saw that Indians he knew were "endowed with the faculties and rights of men, breathing an ardent love of liberty."

This love of liberty eventually began to rub off on the colonists. They had been used to obeying a king, but long association with the liberty-loving Indian people showed them that there was a better way to live. European visitors to America noticed this. A popular book about America, written in Europe in the 1700s said, "The darling passion of the American Indian is liberty and that in its fullest extent; nor is it the original natives only to whom this passion is confined; our colonists sent thither seem to be imbued with the same principles." Clearly such ideas were considered unusual in Europe.

Thomas Jefferson left us definite statements of how he regarded the first Americans and their ways of thinking. His experience and knowledge of Indian people dated back to his boyhood when Indian friends often visited in his parents' home. After he was grown, Jefferson knew and talked with many, both as a private citizen and as a member of the government. In these contacts he found what he called "proofs of genius" in the Native Americans and a "sound understanding." His opinion may be summed up in his words, "I believe the Indian to be in mind and body equal to the white man." This attitude expressed itself clearly in Jefferson's acceptance of many Indian ideals.

Jefferson not only approved of the Indian way of government but declared it to be superior to the kind found in Europe: "Crimes are rare among the Indians; in so much that, were it made a question, whether no law, as among the . . . Americans, or too much law as among the . . . Europeans, submits man to the greatest evil, one who has seen both conditions would pronounce it to be the latter." On another occasion he wrote, "I am convinced that those societies as among the Indians which live without government, enjoy in their general mass an infinitely greater degree of happiness than those who live under European government. Among the former, public opinion is in the place of law, and restrains morals as powerfully as laws ever did anywhere."

Although the Indian people appeared to have little government, they were not lawless. They could live without law, as we understand the word, because each Indian was his or her own law. As Jefferson put it, "Their only controls are their manners and the moral sense of right and wrong, which . . . in every man makes a part of his nature." Jefferson could not bring about a government for the white man in which every citizen's "moral sense of right and wrong" took the place of law. But he approved of such a way of life. And he firmly held the view that citizens should resist the idea of too much government. This view, so commonly held in our country today, may well in part be traced to the many examples set by the Indian cultures.

We can again see the imprint of the Indian democratic tradition in the view that government leaders are public servants and may remain in power only if they carry out the will of the people. The councils and other social structures that guided the affairs of the early Indian societies in peace and war were formed by the people, and those chosen to lead kept their positions only so long as they deserved to do so. This was observed by many white men who lived and traveled among Indian nations north of Mexico in former times. The chief held his office "by superior merit," wrote Meriwether Lewis. The artist George Catlin reported in the early 1800s that the influence of a leader "was gained only by his virtue." Another man wrote that a chief's authority "is only the esteem of the people and ceases the moment that esteem is lost." A colonial governor said of the Iroquois League, "There is not a man in the ministry of the Five Nations who has gained his office otherwise than by merit." Although the white men were acquainted with such principles, they were clearly impressed when they saw the ideas put into practice by the Indians. In our own attitude toward government today, which so resembles that found in many Indian cultures, we owe more to the first Americans than many are willing to admit.

The United States was founded by Europeans, but it is not a copy of Europe. It is a new creation, formed by the cultures of many peoples, of which the heritage of the American Indians is a major part.

CHAPTER

2

Lessons in Conservation from the First Americans

WHEN COLUMBUS reached the homeland of the Indian people, he found the scene so beautiful that he felt possibly he had reached the edge of the earthly Paradise described in the Bible. The Garden of Eden, where the Book of Genesis says Adam and Eve were created, he thought must lie farther inland. The best land in Spain could not compare with this place, he declared in a letter to the king and queen; his eyes never tired of looking at it. He saw a promised land of rich resources and unsurpassed abundance. The explorers and settlers who followed Columbus made the same report, as did later immigrants who traveled westward across the continent. In the Ohio country, in the broad valley of the Mississippi, on the plains, in the mountains, on the western shore, they found clean air, sparkling waters, green grasslands, and fragrant forests. Although further evidence was not needed, artists of the time left their impressions in paintings, which show us the immense, unspoiled beauty and freshness of the land. The first Europeans who entered South America reported the same.

Yet in spite of this, millions of people lived on the two continents at that time, and their ancestors had lived there for at least twenty thousand years—perhaps much longer. The

27

population was not evenly distributed, but the continents were inhabited from the Far North to the southern tip of South America. The agricultural nations of the Incas in the Andes region and the Aztecs in Mexico were the most densely populated. The first Spaniards who entered Mexico reported that the population of the Aztec capital Tenochtitlán (TEEN och teet LAHN) was 300,000 when the explorer Hernando Cortes arrived with his army. The number may have been higher, but even if the city had fewer people, it was still one of the largest cities in the world at the time—perhaps the largest—and more densely populated than Paris or Madrid.

Most Indian people in the Americas used the natural resources of the country, but did so without destroying them. They developed a balanced way of life, in harmony with nature. By protecting and conserving the soil, water, and plant and animal life, they could live in the same region century after century with no ill effects on the environment.

The Inca people of Peru practiced intensive farming over a long period of time, but they did so with great care for the land. Both the Inca and pre-Inca peoples furnished history with an outstanding example of land use. They skillfully cultivated every inch of good soil, maintaining its greatest power to produce. To avoid erosion of the soil, the governments had their engineers build terraces on the steep slopes of the Andes. The field plots of these "staircase farms" were alternate strips of grass and plowed soil. As the rain washed down the mountainside, it was trapped in the grassy ridges, to seep slowly into the strips that were planted. To store water for seasons when it was needed the government built, high in the mountains, rock-lined reservoirs that were fed by glacial streams. These reservoirs were connected with canals and irrigation ducts through which the water could be released, the steepness of the mountain providing power to move the water. After the streams had irrigated the mountainside fields, they ran out to the desert plains to water the crops planted there. These large-scale aqueduct systems,

Sugar Camp by Seth Eastman: women of the Ojibwa (also called Chippewa) and other Indian nations throughout the northeastern lake country of North America tapped maple trees for their sap each spring and boiled the sap down into sugar. Every stage of the work is shown in this painting.

Courtesy James J. Hill Reference Library, St. Paul

built throughout the Inca Empire, are hardly equaled in modern times. The Incas did not invent irrigation, but some historians agree that they perfected it. After more than five hundred years, many of their terraces and canals are still in use.

The Incas made expert and wide use of natural fertilizer. For this they used principally guano (gwAH no), the dung or droppings of sea birds, which lived in immense flocks on islands off the coast. The government made strict regulations protecting the birds, and farmers were permitted to take only as much guano as they needed.

In what is now the American Southwest, Indian people developed a system of irrigation to produce crops of cotton, corn, beans, and squash in their desert homeland. Several miles of canals that are more than two thousand years old still exist in Arizona. Aerial views of the land show that canals once existed there which irrigated a quarter of a million acres.

North of Mexico, much of the area was sparsely populated. There Indian societies adapted their way of life to their surroundings, using the resources as nature directed. Those in the Southwest supported themselves by agriculture. In the area that is now California they learned to use the abundant acorns and other plant products for food. Along the Northwest coast they fished for salmon and took the wood and other products of the forest for their use. Those who made their homes in the Great Plains followed the buffalo herds, which provided them wtih meat to eat and skins for tepees and clothing. Other parts of the animal they made into rope, containers, tools, weapons, and almost everything else they needed. Families who lived in the central forest and lake country hunted game to provide meat and clothing, harvested wild rice, and fished. They took the native birch bark to make their canoes, houses, containers, and other items. The corn and bean farmers living in the Northeast and Southeast added to their crops by hunting and fishing. This way of life had gone on for many centuries when the Europeans arrived, and it could have continued for centuries more.

Although the people who lived north of Mexico differed widely in languages, cultures, and life-styles, in one important respect many of them were alike. They were deeply religious; religion was their way of life. Their religion acknowledged respect not only for human life but for all life, as the creation of the Great Spirit. To the Indians who held this belief the world was a community of human beings, whose rights they respected, and of animals and green growing things that they also respected. They saw every form of life as a part of nature, in which all are related in a brotherhood. "All things are connected. Whatever befalls the earth befalls the sons of the earth," wrote the Dwamish leader Chief Seattle to President Franklin Pierce in 1855. "Whatever happens to the beasts also happens to man. All things share the same breath— the beasts, the trees, the man."

To the Indian, the land was sacred, and life itself was sacred. All forms of life are equal, the Indian believed, and each form has its own kind of work, which must be carried out if all are to survive. Green plants make food, which animals eat. Bees, gathering honey, fertilize the flowers so that they can bear fruits and seeds. Birds and other creatures eat the fruits and spread the plant by returning the seeds to the earth, fertilized by their own waste. Some creatures eat living matter; some—the scavengers—eat dead matter. Tiny organisms in the soil cause dead matter to decay, returning it to the earth, thus completing the life cycle. Native Americans saw themselves as part of nature, depending on the earth and on animals and green growing things for their life. That is why they called other creatures "little brothers"— the four-leggeds and those that swim through the water and fly through the air. When they killed a deer or a bear, they begged the animal's pardon, saying, "Forgive me, little brother, but my people must live." They said the same to the birch trees before taking the bark for a canoe or a house. When they took a plant for food, they said to it, "Your leaves must feed me now, but someday my body will return to the soil to feed your roots."

Because of this reverence for the earth and for all life, the Indians lived in a state of harmony with nature. Their understanding of the world, gained from the experience of day-to-day living, was handed down through the centuries. They felt that they had a right to take only what they needed and no more; they must leave the earth as they found it, for future generations. That is why, when Columbus first saw the land of the New World, it was as beautiful as Paradise.

When the European colonists came to North America, the Indian people were met with an utterly new and strange idea: the white men wanted to buy land—*buy* land. The Native Americans hardly knew how to answer such a request. They laughed. *Buy* land? You might as well want to buy the ocean or a piece of the sky. The land belongs to all life. "As long as the sun shines and the waters flow, this land will be here to give life to men and animals. . . . It was put here by the Great Spirit. We cannot sell it, because it does not belong to us." This kind of talk was repeated hundreds of times as the white men began trying to get land from the Indian people.

The Europeans rejected the Indians' idea about the land, or, more correctly, they never understood it. In Europe land was often owned by the rich and worked by the poor, but it was owned by some person, group, or government. In time, the colonists, and later the pioneer settlers, did acquire Indian land—sometimes by honest purchase, more often by fraud and violence. Then the Indian people were in for another shock as they saw how the white men used the land. In Virginia the colonists planted tobacco on cleared plots, wore out the soil with this crop, and a few years later moved on to other land. Jefferson explained this way of farming by saying that it "does not proceed from lack of knowledge merely; it is from our having such quantities of land to waste as we please. In Europe the object is to make the most of their land, labor being abundant. Here it is to make the most of our labor, land being abundant." Chief Seattle expressed this view well when he wrote that the white man regards one piece of land the same as the next: "He is a stranger who comes in the night and takes from the land whatever he needs. The earth is not his brother but his enemy, and when he has conquered it, he moves on."

The colonists continued to exploit the land and its resources year after year as they forced more and more Indian people from their homes. The fur trade expanded westward, destroyed the wildlife on which the Indians lived, and made them ever more dependent on the white man's goods. Some forms of animal life were entirely wiped out; one was the passenger pigeon, not one of which remains today. This destruction increased as white settlers moved across the continent to the Pacific.

Clearly the white settlers did not use the land as nature intended. To make more fields, they drained swamps and plowed up grasslands. As time passed, they built dams across wide rivers, cut down forests, and stripped off the topsoil to get at minerals buried below. They built cities with factories that dumped chemicals into lakes, rivers, and the air. In the name of progress, they sprayed chemical fertilizers on the fields and used poisons to kill weeds and insects, poisons that have spread around the globe. Today fumes from jet engines and wastes from nuclear power plants and bombs add further destruction.

After centuries of waste and wrong use of natural resources, frightening results are beginning to appear. Residents of some cities are alarmed about the purity of their drinking water. Air alerts warn people to stay indoors because the air is polluted. Green plants in large areas are withering because they are coated with a film of oily dirt. Poisons in rivers and lakes are making fish unfit to eat. Mankind has created problems that never existed before, problems that threaten all life on the earth.

Some people predicted years ago that this would happen if human beings continued to change the natural world into a place of their own making. Those who warned of the present problems are the ecologists, whose science seeks to understand the relationship between the earth and its life forms, and among the many forms of life. Ecology teaches us that all life comes from the earth and depends on the earth, that all forms are related and depend on one another, that each form must be allowed to perform its special task in order for all to live, that mankind cannot disturb any part of the chain of life without affecting every other part. It tells us that human beings must care for nature, of which they are part, or they will destroy themselves.

But is this not the truth that the Indians of North America recognized ages ago and are still maintaining? Indeed, the Indian people have been called America's first ecologists. We are now forced to recognize their ideas as the only principles that will preserve life.

Although the white man and the rest of the world have taken much from the first Americans, in this area it is clear that much is left to be learned. The Indians' recognition of man's place in nature has been called one of their greatest gifts to the rest of the world. But it is a gift that we must accept if we are to benefit.

John Collier, United States Commissioner of Indian Affairs in the 1930s, wrote of the Indian people, "They had what the world has lost. What the world has lost, the world must have again, lest it die. . . . It is the lost reverence and passion for human personality, joined with the ancient lost reverence for the earth and its web of life." When the Europeans came to America five hundred years ago, the Indians taught them how to survive. Their teachings are needed today more than ever.

CHAPTER
3
Indian Help for the First Europeans in the Americas

THE FIRST human beings arrived in the Americas many thousands of years ago. Some think they may have come over a land bridge which then stretched between northeast Asia and Alaska. If so, they were the ones who discovered America. These ancient peoples entered the Western Hemisphere when human culture all over the world was in a very early stage. Agriculture had not been invented, and men had not yet domesticated any animal except the dog. The wandering newcomers entered a land where no one had ever lived. The country may not have been very different from the place they left, but it was new to them. They did not know where rivers led, where edible plants grew, what animals lived there and which ones might be dangerous or useful. Gradually exploring farther, through thousands of years, they made themselves at home on the two continents.

The greatest work of exploring had been done when the Europeans began coming to the Americas in the late 1400s. To the white men, however, the land was new and strange, even dangerous. They were not even sure where they were on the globe; they saw people unlike any they had seen before. Columbus and his men, like the explorers who came after them, needed help almost as soon as they landed. Fortunately for them, many of the people they found could, and would, help them. In fact, the first Indians Columbus met were so kind and generous that he could hardly believe it. His account says, "Of anything they possess, if it be asked of them, they never say no."

These people at once and repeatedly offered Columbus and his men food and also helped them in other ways. When sailors went ashore to look for fresh water, Native Americans led them to the springs and even carried the full casks back to the boats. When groups explored on land, the Indians carried the Spaniards on their backs through swamps and across rivers. The Spanish took cruel advantage of this goodness. Columbus said later that he found the Indians "fit to be ordered around and made to work." When his ship the *Santa Maria* was wrecked off the coast of one of the islands, Indian men helped the sailors build a fort out of boards salvaged from the boat. While supplies were taken off the wreck, it was Indians who kept watch both on board and on the beach to see that nothing was stolen. Columbus could trust them more than he could his own treacherous and greedy sailors. On other occasions Indians rescued Spaniards who became lost in the forests, taught them how to prepare native foods, and gave the expedition supplies.

From the start, what Columbus needed most was guides. He believed that he had reached Asia, and he wanted to find Japan. He was also eager to find gold to take back to the king and queen of Spain, who had paid for his expedition. Since he had no idea in which direction to sail, the explorer captured several Indian men and—after he had taught them some Spanish—forced them to serve as guides and interpreters. These men were only the first of many whom Columbus took on board for this purpose. When the ships reached an area where the captives did not know the language, Columbus released the men and took others to serve him. Columbus seemed pleased with this way of getting information. One account says that the Indians "learned Spanish with surprising rapidity." Another calls one of the inter-preters "intelligent and useful." The Europeans gained valuable knowledge through these guides and interpreters, knowledge that would otherwise have been difficult to come by. Columbus was only the first explorer to use the Indians in this way.

On Columbus's last voyage, which began in 1502, Indians helped save his life and the lives of his men. When sailing in the Caribbean Sea, the admiral's two ships began to leak so badly that they were no longer seaworthy and had to be run ashore on the island of Jamaica. There they stayed. To get help, several leaders of the expedition started out in two Indian dugout canoes, each with six sailors and ten Indian paddlers. Their destination was the Spanish colony on the island of Hispaniola, which lay across a hundred miles of rough, open water. Several Indian men lost their lives in that disastrous voyage; the rest may never have been able to re-turn home. But the dugouts did reach Hispaniola, where the men finally obtained a ship that took Columbus and the re-maining men from Jamaica back to Europe.

A good many European explorers did not return from their voyages to the Americas but died of shipwreck, disease, star-vation, and other calamities. Of those who did survive and accomplish their purposes, many owed their lives to the help of Indians. Amerigo Vespucci, shipwrecked off the coast of Brazil in 1497, was rescued by men who, when they saw his plight, "went out in their little boats . . . carried ashore the men and the munitions which were contained therein, with charity so great that it is impossible to describe." The Span-ish explorer Cabeza de Vaca and his men, blown ashore on an island off the coast of Texas in 1528, were rescued, fed, and otherwise helped by Native Americans living there. These are only a few of what must be hundreds of examples of how the American Indians helped the first European in-vaders in their lands.

The fate of the early colonists was, if anything, even more

uncertain than that of the explorers. Those people had to come prepared to stay, sending their ships back to Europe. The first English colonists on the Atlantic coast were pitifully small groups surrounded by wilderness and strangers. For them, especially, the Indian people held the key to survival. Conditions for the first colonies were so difficult that several colonizing attempts failed. Some Europeans, not able to bear the hardships of getting established on distant foreign soil, sailed back home.

The first English colonists to succeed—and they almost failed—were the ones who founded Jamestown, Virginia, in 1607. Those people admitted before they started out that they did not know how to prepare themselves for the life they would face. "What wee shoulde finde, what we should want, where we should bee, we were all ignorant," says one of their records. They had expected to make the ocean crossing in two months, arriving in America in time to plant fields in the spring. Instead, "we were at sea five months, where we both spent our vituall [food] and lost the opportunity of the time and the season to plant." The writer of that account admitted there was "nothing so difficult as to establish a common wealth so farre from men and meanes." But the "men and meanes" of the Indian "common wealth" surrounded them, and without that, they might well have perished during their first year in America.

Of the more than one hundred Jamestown colonists who arrived in May 1607, nearly half had died by the end of summer. Their food supply dwindled, and they had little success in adding to it. Finally, when they had almost nothing left, neighboring Indians came to the rescue, bringing them corn. The account written by the colonist Captain John Smith says they brought corn "ere it was half ripe, to refresh us, when we rather expected . . . they would destroy us." Their benefactor was Powhatan, a powerful Indian leader, who with his men could easily have wiped out the little settlement.

Later, when the colonists were again in want, Smith wrote, "Our provisions being now within twentie dayes spent, the Indians brought us great store both of corne and bread ready made." Another time he wrote that the colony was so destitute, "that had not the Indians fed us, we directly had starved."

When the colonists grew in numbers, they began to threaten the Indians and force them to give or sell them food. Powhatan answered one such threat by saying, "Why will you take by force what is gladly given?" The colonists answered with more force. Forty years after the first Virginians had arrived, they had driven Powhatan and his people from their homes and taken their lands.

The Indians did more than give the settlers corn, beans, and other provisions. They taught the newcomers how to provide their own crops. In the spring of 1609, Smith persuaded two captive Indians to show the colonists how to plant corn. Forty acres were thus planted under Indian supervision and instruction. Not until the colonists were established agriculturally was their future secure. At first the only products they could depend on were the native plants such as corn, beans, and squash.

An American crop that came to be of great importance to the Virginia colony was tobacco. Tobacco grew in the area of Jamestown, and the colonists learned from the Indians how to raise it. The crop did so well in Virginia that it saved the colony from bankruptcy. Indeed, in a few years, Virginia prospered greatly because of the tobacco harvests.

The situation of the Plymouth colonists, who arrived in 1620, was as desperate as that of the Virginians. William Bradford, a member of the Plymouth company, wrote of his fellow Pilgrims, "If they looked behind them, ther was the mighty ocean which they had passed, and was now as a main barr and goulfe." And ahead "what could they see but a hideous and desolate wilderness?" Their fears were not unfounded. Of the hundred or so who landed in December 1620, nearly half died during the first winter from disease and hardship.

Besides suffering from sickness and hunger, the little group at first lived in constant fear of the Americans. Yet these Pilgrims benefited from Indian gifts even before they had made a permanent landing. It came about in this way. Before deciding on the place where they would settle, the Pilgrims sailed along the coast in the *Mayflower* stopping at various places to inspect the land. At one place where a group went ashore to look around, they found a field of "new stubble where corn had been set, the same year." There, too, they found "heaps of sand, newly paddled with their hands." The men anxiously dug into these piles and found "fair Indian baskets filled with corn . . . which seemed to them a goodly sight, having never seen any such before." The Pilgrims took some of the grain and reburied the rest. When they returned to the *Mayflower,* those on the ship "were marvelously glad and their hearts encouraged." Later the Pilgrims paid the Indians for this corn that they took.

During the first weeks they were on American soil, the Plymouth colonists saw little of the Indians. But the Indians were watching them, planning how to approach the invaders and deal with them. Although the colonists lived in great fear of the Americans, the Indians in turn also mistrusted the strange-looking, bearded white men. They had reason to fear the intruders, for Indians had been killed or kidnapped by Europeans exploring the coastal waters in sailing vessels.

Two months after the Pilgrims landed, an Indian messenger appeared in their village. To the amazement of the colonists this man, named Samoset, spoke to them in English, a language he had learned from fishermen and seamen cruising along the shore. Far from being a danger to the Pilgrims, Samoset "became profitable to them in acquainting them with many things concerning the state of the country . . . as also of the people."

Samoset departed after a day and a night, to return later with five companions and announce that their leader, Massasoit, was not far off and would visit the colony. After a few days Massasoit appeared, accompanied by sixty warriors. One member of the company was Squanto, who probably knew more English than any other Indian in North America at that time.

Squanto had been kidnapped once, possibly twice, and taken onto English ships. Although the records of his experiences are incomplete, it is known that he spent some years in England and was helpful to several English explorers. In 1619 Squanto returned to the area of Plymouth, his original home. By that time not only could he speak English but he also knew the English people and what to expect from them.

Squanto was the ideal interpreter for Massasoit; he could also advise the leader how to deal with the foreigners. After an exchange of gifts and some entertainment, the Indian leader and the principal men of Plymouth colony made an agreement of peace and friendship—what we today might call a mutual assistance pact. This agreement was honored by both sides and lasted until the death of Massasoit many years later.

After the Plymouth-Massasoit "summit meeting," all the Indians departed except Squanto, who stayed in the colony. Squanto's help to the Pilgrams is well known. Bradford says in his history of the colony that Squanto "continued with them and was their interpreter and was a special instrument sent of God for their good, beyond their expectation. He directed them how to set their corn, where to take fish, and to procure other commodities, and was also their pilot to bring them to unknown places for their profit and never left them." When spring came, the colonists who were well enough to work "began to plant their corn, in which service Squanto stood them in great stead showing them both the manner how to set it, and after how to dress and tend it. Also he told them, except they got fish and set with it in these old grounds it would come to nothing. And he also showed them . . . how to get other provisions necessary for them. All which they found true by trial and experience."

The Pilgrims were almost entirely dependent on Squanto and Massasoit for their food and safety for more than two years. Even then, they were still in danger of starvation and want. Their own crops were not enough to see them through the third winter, and they lived off corn and beans traded from people whom Squanto had led them to. These Indians actually let the colonists have more food than they could spare.

After Squanto's death Hobomok, another one of Massasoit's men, became their guide and helper. Squanto and Hobomok taught the Pilgrims how to catch fish, take and prepare clams, stalk and trap game, tap the maple trees for sap, grind corn and make bread, bake beans, prepare pumpkins for the winter, and develop dozens of other skills.

When American schools and historians honor the Pilgrim fathers, they should include Squanto, Massasoit, and Hobomok. If it had not been for the help of these and other Indian people, the Pilgrims might well have died of starvation and never been heard of again.

After several colonies had been established on the Atlantic coast, the settlements began to be of some help to one another. But the accounts of William Penn, Roger Williams, John Smith, and other colonial leaders show that help from the first Americans still played a great part in the welfare of their communities. Even a century later a British government agent, whose work was dealing with the Native Americans, said, "The importance of the Indians is now generally known and understood. A doubt remains not, that the prosperity of our colonies on the continent, will stand or fall with our interest and favor among them."

Many Indian people at first believed that the Europeans were only visitors. Eventually they realized that the for-

Indian women taught the early settlers how to make maple sugar. Non-Indian people continue the practice today in many of the same groves, using Indian methods. This Currier and Ives print pictures a pioneer New England maple sugar camp.

Courtesy Heritage Plantation, Sandwich, Massachusetts

eigners had come to stay and that they would take away their lands. This led to many bitter conflicts. Sometimes the Indians battled the intruders, trying to save their homes and families. Sometimes the white men attacked the Indians and drove them away. Yet after many white people had shown themselves to be hostile, Native Americans in many areas continued to help them and even rescue them from death. When settlement began to spread westward from the Atlantic, Indian people became helpful in new ways, often actually making it easier for the invaders to take over the lands that had been their home for so long.

Part II

CHAPTER
4
Indian Trails and the Conquest of the Americas

By 1492, when the first Europeans arrived in the New World, the Indian people had, through centuries of experience, learned to know the forests, the deserts and mountains, the seashores and plains of the Americas. They had discovered the lowest mountain passes, the safest places to cross rivers, the shortest and easiest portage routes between bodies of water. They wore paths along the rivers to use when the streams were too shallow for boats, and they established portage paths around waterfalls and from one waterway to another. They often followed the pathways of buffalo and elk, gradually extending their routes of travel farther and farther across the continents. In Mexico and Peru the Indian nations built great highway systems. Both there and in the rest of the Americas they eventually covered the land with a network of trails.

On these Indian roads the European invaders entered the Americas, first to explore, then to trade and conquer, and finally to settle. In the 1500s the Spanish conquistadores invaded Mexico and South America on Indian highways that took them over the continents. The French who sailed up the St. Lawrence River during the 1600s and 1700s followed the forest pathways in the Great Lakes region and westward to carry on the fur trade with Indian people and claim the land for France. Native Americans guided the French explorer and geographer Samuel de Champlain up the Ottawa River to Georgian Bay along trails that later became part of the highway system of the province of Ontario. Other Indians guided the fur trader Henry Kelsey from Hudson Bay to the edge of the Canadian prairie along their trails. The explorer and fur trader Alexander Mackenzie followed Indian paths to become the first white man to cross Canada.

Moving inland from the Atlantic coast, the first traders, missionaries, soldiers, and settlers came to rely for their safety and guidance on the thoroughfares of the Indian people. Even those who claimed to be discoverers were most often led by Indian guides along Indian pathways. After the explorers, the traders led their packhorses along the narrow traces. In the 1700s the routes were widened for the wagons of armies and pioneers. By the mid-1800s settlers were still moving west, but they were using a new form of transportation—the railroad. Then the ancient traces, which had served the white man's purpose for packhorses, mule trains, covered wagons, and stagecoaches, again proved their worth. Some of them were now followed by the rails, beginning in the East and moving ever farther westward.

In the early 1900s, with the invention of the automobile, many of the age-old trails were made into modern highways. If we traced them to their beginnings, we would find that not only some state and federal highways but also hundreds of county and country roads follow courses once chosen by Indian people.

Our debt to the Indian for these pathways is well expressed in the words of Peter Wilson, an Iroquois leader, who told white men in 1847: "The Empire State, as you love to call it, was once laced by our trails from Albany to Buffalo; trails that we had trodden for centuries; trails worn so deep by the feet of the Iroquois that they became your roads of travel, as your possessions gradually ate into those of my people.

The IROQUOIS TRAIL

NAMES of CITIES and
NAMES and BORDERS
of STATES ARE MODERN.

++++ Conrail System
----- New York Thruway
····· Iroquois Trail

25 50 Miles
   50 100 Kilometers

Your roads still traverse the same lines of commerce which once bound one part of the Long House to the other. Have we, the early possessors of this land, no part in your history?"

When settlers began to invade Indian lands west of the Appalachians, even before the American Revolution, most of them reached the Ohio Basin by traveling along great Indian trails that led into the interior of the continent.

Farthest north, the old Iroquois Trail, running across the state of New York, is one of those mentioned by the Iroquois leader who asked, "Have we no part in your history?" This route passed through the territory of the famous Iroquois League—which the white men called the Long House—from Albany on the Hudson River to Buffalo on Lake Erie. In the French and Indian Wars and later during revolutionary times this trail, made into a roadway, became a major route for colonial armies. Afterward it served as one of the main highways for pioneer settlers going to the Ohio Valley. In the early 1800s the road became the route of the Erie Canal, joining the waters of Lake Erie and the Hudson River. The

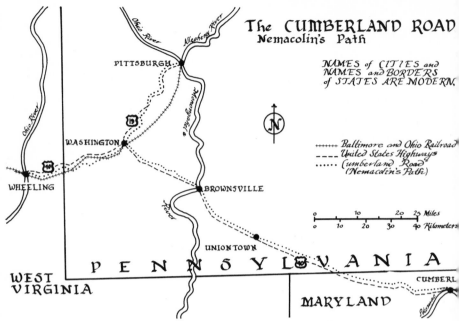

The CUMBERLAND ROAD
Nemacolin's Path

NAMES of CITIES and
NAMES and BORDERS
of STATES ARE MODERN.

PITTSBURGH

WASHINGTON

WHEELING

BROWNSVILLE

++++++ Baltimore and Ohio Railroad
---- United States Highways
...... Cumberland Road
(Nemacolin's Path)

0   10   20   25 Miles
0   10   20   30   40 Kilometers

UNIONTOWN

PENNSYLVANIA

WEST
VIRGINIA

MARYLAND

CUMBERL

trail did further service when a railroad line, now part of the
Conrail Corporation, was built along the route. Today the
New York State Thruway runs along the old trail.

A second major route from the Atlantic coast followed an
ancient Indian road from Cumberland, Maryland, on the
Potomac River to Pittsburgh where the Allegheny and Mo-
nongahela rivers join to form the Ohio. This path proved
so valuable for early travelers that they hired the Indian
leader Nemacolin to mark it for them. And so at first it was
called Nemacolin's Path. During the French and Indian Wars
the English made it into a military road. The first English
army to enter the West was led over this trail by a young
officer named George Washington. Later a branch of the
road was built to follow a trail from Washington, Pennsylvania, to the Ohio River at Wheeling, West Virginia. The
route from Cumberland to Wheeling, made into a federal
highway in the early 1800s, took the name of the Cumberland Road. This Indian path became one of the great
thoroughfares in United States history, the principal route
joining the eastern seacoast with the interior. One of the
nation's first rail lines was built along the Cumberland Road.

Now the Baltimore and Ohio railroad line follows the old trail part of the way from Pittsburgh to Wheeling. U.S. Highway 40 follows the trail from Cumberland to Wheeling. The section of Nemacolin's Path from Washington to Pittsburgh is now U.S. Highway 19.

The third major trail through the mountain barrier was the Wilderness Road. This great overland trail was a section of the Indian trace known as the Warriors' Path, which extended south from the Potomac in West Virginia, through Virginia, and crossed the Appalachian Mountains at Cumberland Gap. That famous pass at the western tip of Virginia is a natural opening in the mountains which both the Indian and the buffalo found in ancient times. Like the Cumberland Road, this route was used by traders who wanted it marked and opened, fallen trees removed and streams bridged. Clearing a 200-mile stretch of the route was undertaken in 1775 by the frontier scout Daniel Boone. He and his crew approached the gap from the east near Gate City, Virginia, along a trail that is now U.S. Highway 58. West of the Gap they followed the trail for 50 miles, then turned north. A road built later, continued along the Warriors' Path westward from that point through Danville to Louisville, on the

The WARRIORS' PATH ~ Wilderness Road

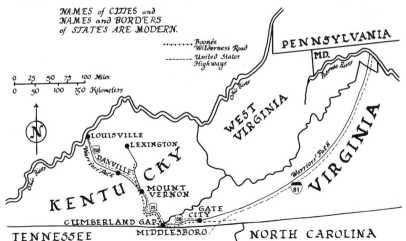

Ohio. Before long so many eager settlers jammed Boone's road through the mountains that in 1792 Kentucky joined the Union as the first state west of the Appalachians. At first only the section cleared by Boone was called the Wilderness Road. Later the name was applied to the whole route from the Potomac to Louisville. Those traveling U.S. Highway 150 today from Mount Vernon through Danville to Louisville are following that Indian road. U.S. Highway 25 roughly follows the trail from Cumberland Gap to near Lexington. Interstate 81 has been built along the eastern stretch of the Warriors' Path from the Tennessee border to the Potomac.

Many other Indian roads proved valuable to the people of the growing United States as they seized Indian land ever farther westward, finally reaching the fertile plains of the Mississippi Valley. When they had invaded the Middle West by way of Indian paths, they used the same means to go to the Rockies and beyond, to the Far West.

The Big Medicine Trail is the great Indian thoroughfare by which the invading white men found their way from the Mississippi to the mouth of the Columbia at the Pacific. This overland route, later known as the Oregon Trail, was first traversed by white men when the Scottish fur trader Robert Stuart and six companions traveled eastward from the mouth of the Columbia to St. Louis in 1812 and 1813. From the Pacific, he and his men paddled up the Columbia to the Snake River. There they traded with Cayuse Indians for twelve horses and set out along well-worn Indian paths across northeastern Oregon to an upper section of that river. Following the Snake across southern Idaho, they came to the Portneuf River. This they followed south, then struck out eastward to the Bear River. Their aim was to find a mountain pass that would take them across the Rockies to the plains beyond. Stuart was told by an Indian guide that there was a pass "to the south" that led through the mountains. This was undoubtedly the South Pass, later a famous point in the Oregon Trail.

Stuart and his men were wholly dependent on Indian paths. Of one trail Stuart wrote, "Although to us an unknown road, we trusted it." Following the Bear River into western Wyoming, they wanted to continue straight east to the pass in the Rockies that the guide had told Stuart about. But threatened by Crow Indians they fled north on an Indian trace. The men who had threatened them caught up with them one morning and drove off their horses, leaving them to proceed on foot. After a lengthy detour Stuart and his men headed east once more into the mountains. Nearly starving, they came upon a group of Snake Indian hunters who kindly fed and sheltered the party, even sold them their only horse. Again following Indian pathways the Stuart expedition made its way "to a gap discernible in the mountains in the southeast direction." This was the pass they had been looking for. They crossed the Continental Divide here, over a deep Indian path, and emerged into the region where the waters flow eastward. Passing along the Sweetwater River, they reached the North Platte. From there, the way was easy. They trudged along the Platte until they came to the Missouri, then floated downstream in canoes to St. Louis. History books may say that Stuart "discovered" the Oregon Trail, but the route he "discovered" had been traversed by Indian people for thousands of years.

Because of their forced detour, Stuart and his men did not travel the stretch between Bear River in southeastern Idaho and the South Pass. This section was covered by trappers not long afterward. As news spread of the rich furs that Stuart had found in the Rockies, frontiersmen hastily loaded packhorses with traps and flocked westward over the plains. Within ten years of Stuart's journey, these mountain men had explored every stream and valley in the region in their search for beaver. During the 1830s the entire route that would be called the Oregon Trail became as familiar to the mountain men as it had been for many centuries to the Indians. By the end of the decade, a well-defined, continuous road extended 2,000 miles from Independence, Missouri, to western Oregon. This meant that families, traveling in wagons, could now make the trip to the Pacific. It was not long before they began to do so, in great numbers, mountain men acting as guides for the overland caravans. Council Bluffs, Iowa, and St. Joseph and Independence, Missouri, were favorite points where the wagon trains assembled to begin the long trek. By the 1840s thousands each year traversed the Indians' Big Medicine Trail to the Northwest. There white families settled where Indian men, women, and children had made their homes for many centuries, but from which they had been driven away.

The Oregon Trail was not a narrow trace marked by a set of wagon-wheel tracks, as some people imagine. As more wagons, horses, mules, oxen, and cattle traversed the route, the trail began to spread out, in open country becoming as much as 20 miles wide. Travelers veered to left and right as they sought fresh water, firewood, or grazing land for

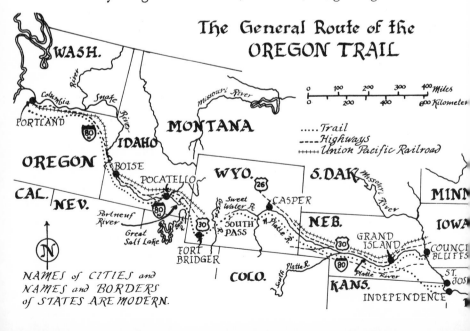

The General Route of the OREGON TRAIL

..... Trail
---- Highways
++++ Union Pacific Railroad

NAMES of CITIES and NAMES and BORDERS of STATES ARE MODERN.

their livestock. Others looked for shortcuts or made little detours. The strands of the trail came together at mountain passes, at fording places over deep rivers, and at forts built by the mountain men.

Today no highway or railroad follows the varied windings of the Oregon Trail continuously. Several modern transportation routes do, however, use parts of the old Indian road. The rails of the Union Pacific follow the Platte–North Platte River section through most of Nebraska and again from western Wyoming, through Idaho, across Oregon to Portland. Interstate highways 80 and 80-N lead along almost identical stretches. U.S. Highway 30 takes the trail through Nebraska, and 26 follows it into eastern Wyoming. In western Wyoming Highway 30 follows the Bear River route to the Snake River in Idaho and joins 80-N to continue to the Pacific. After a century and a half, the wagon ruts of the Oregon Trail have grown dim and almost vanished, but the great route made by the Indian people still leads men and women across the continent.

Just as Indian roads in large measure determined where the white invaders traveled over the continent from the time of their arrival until the present, in like manner the location of Indian villages, on Indian trails, determined where many of the white men's trading posts and army forts were built, later to be replaced by settlements, some of which grew into cities.

Dozens of large and small communities in our nation stand on sites which Indian people in ancient times selected for fresh water, shelter from winds, and nearness to important crossroads and waterways. Council Bluffs, Iowa, stands on such a spot. Louisville, Kentucky, was built on an Indian trail. Fort Duquesne—later Fort Pitt, still later Pittsburgh—was built at a point where important trails came together. Detroit, Chicago, and Kansas City are located where once burned the village fires of the first Americans. The early growth and importance of Akron, Ohio, is due to its location on a portage path that crossed a main watershed highway of ancient times. St. Louis is located where once stood an Indian community. The settlers of the Massachusetts colony founded Springfield and other communities along Indian pathways. Many other examples could be given.

Even the streets in some cities were once Indian trails. Main Street in Los Angeles is such a street. Hennepin Avenue, a major thoroughfare in Minneapolis, Minnesota, follows mainly an Indian trace leading from a lake in the city to the Falls of St. Anthony in the Mississippi. Mound Street in St. Louis is so named because it was once a pathway leading to an Indian mound.

Few people know the important part which Indian people had in determining the location of our highways, railroads, and cities. We are telling only half the story if we do not remember this fact. Let us acknowledge that, in this respect, the "early possessors of our land" indeed have an important part in our history.

CHAPTER
5

Foods from the Indians: Peanuts, Chocolate, Chewing Gum, Baked Beans, and Others

OF ALL THE STRANGE things the first Europeans found in the Americas, the plants must have seemed the strangest. The newcomers had never seen corn, potatoes, peanuts, tomatoes, or pineapples, and many others, nor did most Europeans at first realize the importance of the plants. They looked on them as curiosities. The Spanish conquerors were after the gold of the Aztecs and the Incas; the French traders came for rich furs from the northern tribes; the English settlers wanted land. None of the Europeans came to America in search of food. Before long, however, they began to realize that Indian food could save their lives. In time, they came to see the wealth that lay in the New World crops.

Some readers might think that, since potatoes, corn, beans, and other plants grew in the Americas, the white men would have found them even if there had been no Indians here to show them. Not so. The Indians found these plants in their wild forms many thousands of years earlier and domesticated them to a state of usefulness and importance. If no one had been living in the Americas, the first colonists would have used only the seeds and plants that they had brought from Europe, which they knew how to cultivate: wheat, barley, turnips, carrots, cabbage, and others. The scrubby little wild plants, which would have been undeveloped if there had been no Indian people, would almost certainly have gone unrecognized and might have been lost to the world. Even if some or most of the important plants had been discovered and developed by the Europeans, the process would have taken many years, even with modern scientific methods. As it was, the Europeans found corn and other foods ready to be used when they arrived.

How did it happen that the first Americans developed such a large number of food crops and other plants that have

This 9-inch pottery jar in the form of corn ears came from the Chimú civilization that flourished in Peru five centuries ago, yet the corn ears that form the jar look much like the corn that is raised in our fields today.
Courtesy Museum of the American Indian, Heye Foundation

proved so valuable? Some of the story can be pieced together.

When the first people wandered into the Americas from somewhere in the Eastern Hemisphere, at least twenty thousand years ago, all people on earth were still living on fish, game, and other wild foods. The first Americans did not know, when they traveled to the Western Hemisphere, that they would lose some of the foods they had enjoyed in the eastern half of the world. Among them were wild grains such as the wheat and barley that grew in Upper Egypt, Asia Minor, and other parts of the Eastern Hemisphere and that needed only to be harvested. Many kinds of wild animals roamed the Eastern Hemisphere—horses, cows, sheep, pigs, goats, and other creatures. The primitive tribes there domesticated these animals, which then served them in various ways. By contrast, almost no animals in the Western Hemisphere were worth domesticating. Lacking the advantages they would have had in the Eastern Hemisphere, the first Americans made the most of what they found in their new home. The results were unusual. Historians generally agree that Indian people, especially those in Mexico and Peru, showed the greatest talent of any people in early history for domesticating plants.

Whether American agriculture started first in Mexico or in Peru is not known, but farmers in the Andes Mountains were raising squash, peppers, and beans as much as eight thousand years ago. Potatoes were also among the vegetables grown there in very early times. We know this because, in ancient graves in Peru, pottery has been found that was formed in the shape of vegetables like those grown in our own gardens today. Some of the same crops were also raised in Mexico. The ancient Mexican and South American farmers developed these crops from wild plants: corn possibly from one or two highland grasses that grew in Mexico, potatoes from a wild nightshade that can still be found in the Andes, beans from stringy vines, sweet potatoes from a morning-glory plant.

There are no records to tell us how the early Indians domesticated plants. Some plant changes may have been accidents of nature. Others were certainly brought about by the skill of men and women who carefully saved seeds or fruits from each harvest, choosing those that had characteristics they wanted to preserve. Some seeds might have been taken to a very dry or cool region where they were planted. The few seeds that would mature were then planted for the next harvest. In this way the Indian farmers developed varieties of the same plant that would grow well in hot or cold lands, in dry or wet areas, and in many kinds of soil. No plants of the Old World can grow in as many different climates as those of the New World. Care, patience, and never-ending interest in improvements and methods were needed to domesticate crops, through generations of plants and generations of those who planted.

In this way American Indian farmers and gardeners domesticated as many as forty plants for use as food, fiber, and medicine. At least twenty of them have proved to be of value to the world, and a few of very great value. It is a tribute to the first American planters that in the five hundred years since white men first came to the New World, the most expert scientists have not found a single plant of any importance on the two continents that had not been discovered and developed by the Indians. New varieties and hybrids have been created since then, but not one new bean or potato, for instance, that the most ancient Mexicans or Peruvians would not recognize at once.

These foods all came into world use in much the same way. Each was seen or eaten by European explorers who learned about it from Indian people. They took the foods back to Europe, where some were accepted rapidly, some more slowly. Historical records tell us how their use spread farther and farther. For centuries, however, Indian people were given little or no credit for these gifts to the rest of the world. Botanists in Europe were sure that the plants originated in the Eastern Hemisphere. Sometimes accidents of history gave false names to the plants—like Irish potatoes, Turkish tobacco, Egyptian cotton, and Spanish peanuts. Yet the early records as well as careful research in more recent times tell us clearly that all these plants came from the American Indians.

Among the oldest vegetables are squash, pumpkins, avocados, and peppers. They were widely raised in the Americas when the Europeans arrived. On the Atlantic coast, Indians introduced the colonists to squash and pumpkins and taught them how to grow and prepare the vegetables. The Spaniards quickly adopted the avocado, a Mexican food. By the 1600s, peppers were being raised in many gardens in Europe.

There are two kinds of American pepper. The sweet mild variety is used raw in salads and may be stuffed and baked. When ripe, it is used to stuff olives or dried and powdered to make paprika. This spice, often called Hungarian paprika, is of course another Indian food. The spicy red peppers may flavor chili con carne or be dried and ground to make cayenne pepper.

Sweet potatoes are among the most valuable foods given to the world by the first Americans. Columbus and his men liked the vegetable so much that on his first visit the admiral laid in a supply for the return voyage. By the early 1500s the Spanish were raising sweet potatoes in the West Indies to feed sailors sailing between Europe and America. Spanish and Portuguese ships took the vegetables to the Orient where it has become an important food. Sweet potatoes are today the world's leading root crop. (The white potato is not a root, but the swollen end of an underground stem.) This Indian plant is one of the main foods in the southern United States, Central and South America, India, Africa, and especially China and Japan. It may surprise you to learn that in Japan the sweet potato is second in importance only to rice.

Common beans—green beans, kidney beans, wax beans,

and others—were being raised in Mexico and South America as much as eight thousand years ago. Lima beans take their name from the capital city of Peru. By the 1500s varieties of beans had been developed that grew in many regions on the two continents. English colonists saw the vegetables growing in the Indians' cornfields and soon learned to depend on them. It is from the Indians that they learned to prepare baked beans like the kind we eat today. In time, beans of many kinds became a regular part of the world's diet. The United States government has fed beans to millions of men and women in the armed forces. The common white kidney bean has been eaten by so many sailors that it has become known as the navy bean.

The tomato, another Indian food, is the most widely used vegetable in America today, next to the potato. It is the vegetable most often canned and processed. The first Spaniards in the New World found large fields of tomatoes growing in Mexico, and some of the conquistadores liked the strange fruit. An early Spanish historian described tomatoes as "colde and very wholesome, a kind of graine, great and full of juice, the which gives a good taste to sauce, and they are goode to eat." One could hardly express it better. Of course the tomato is not a "graine" but neither is it a vegetable, although that is what we usually call it. It is a fruit. Tomatoes were taken to Europe in 1544, but were rejected because people there thought they were poison. Thomas Jefferson raised them in his garden, but he was ahead of his time in many things. It is hard to believe that not until the early 1800s were tomatoes commonly eaten in the United States and Europe. Now they are raised and enjoyed in most countries where the climate is suitable for their growth.

Chocolate is another delicious food that we owe to the American Indians. Spanish explorers found groves of chocolate trees growing in Peru, when they arrived there in the early 1500s. Chocolate was also raised in the lush tropics of Yucatán, long before Columbus found the beaches of the

West Indies. Chocolate was an important product among the Aztecs, who obtained it in trade with the Mayas. The seeds were often used as money. Hernando Cortes and his soldiers in the Aztec capital saw the emperor Montezuma drinking foaming chocolate from a golden goblet. It may have been a bitter drink, flavored with vanilla and ground spices, although the Aztecs sometimes sweetened the drink with honey. After tasting it himself, Cortes took chocolate back to Spain. There no one cared for the strange Indian food until a member of the Spanish court had the idea of adding sugar to the drink. Then chocolate became very popular—among royalty and the rich, who could afford it.

Chocolate and cocoa, more correctly cacao (kah KAH o), are made from the seeds of a tropical American plant. Indian people learned long ago to ferment and roast the seeds, then grind them, thus creating the chocolate flavor. The process produces a brown solid that we know as chocolate. Cocoa is made by grinding the solid and pressing out some of the oil. How did the American Indians invent the process for creating chocolate? The answer is lost in history. Today the most up-to-date methods of manufacture cannot improve on it.

Chocolate was first manufactured in the American colonies in 1765 out of seeds brought from the West Indies. Its use has increased steadily since then. Today most chocolate is raised in West Africa and in tropical regions of the Americas, but chocolate products are known and enjoyed around the world. Carolus Linnaeus, the eighteenth-century Swedish botanist who named and classified the world's plants, must have liked the taste of chocolate, for he gave this Indian food a Greek name that means "food for the gods." Few people would disagree with his choice.

Vanilla is another discovery or invention of the Indians. We know that the Aztecs were using domesticated vanilla pods in the early 1500s, so they must have cultivated the vine long before. The flavoring that we know as vanilla is made from the long, thin pods of the vanilla vine. The pods, which have little taste when they are picked, must be cured or fermented and then dried to produce the vanilla flavor. The extract is made by crushing them. It requires great skill to cultivate the vanilla plant. Just as much skill is required to cure and dry the pods, a process that takes four to five months. Another difficulty in making vanilla arises because of the size of the flower. Since the vanilla flower is small, it can be fertilized only by a certain very small Mexican bee that is not always present. For this reason, present-day growers carry out the fertilizing process by hand. Did the ancient Indians do this as well? If so, they must have understood the process of hand fertilization and may have used the same method with other plants to produce the kinds of crops they wanted.

Vanilla was first mentioned in print in an account written by one of Cortes's officers. He wrote that vanilla pods were among the more costly tributes brought to the Aztec emperor. The Aztecs valued the flavoring agent so highly that they refused to share it with others. After the Spanish discovered it, they took vanilla pods back to Spain. By the late 1500s both chocolate and vanilla were being made in Spanish factories. Today vanilla vines are raised in Mexico and Puerto Rico as well as in Madagascar and other tropical areas of of the world, and this American Indian flavoring is enjoyed in many lands.

The French explorers and traders who came to the St. Lawrence Valley in the early 1600s were the first white people to learn about maple syrup, another delightful food that we owe to the Indians, to those who made their homes in forests around the Great Lakes and in the regions that are now eastern Canada and the northeastern United States. Indians showed the French traders and later the settlers how to make maple sugar by tapping the trees in spring, gathering the sap, and boiling it down.

Maple syrup and sugar are made from several kinds of

maple trees that grow nowhere in the world except in north-eastern North America extending west as far as Minnesota. There today, in many of the same groves, people still make maple sugar, using Indian methods. A small but valuable industry makes maple products that are enjoyed throughout the United States and Canada. Part of each year's crop is sent to Europe.

An important Indian food that people in temperate climates know little about has several names of which manioc and cassava are the most common. It is another crop from the American tropics. Manioc, a shrub, has roots that taste something like sweet potatoes and are rich in food value. There are two kinds of manioc, the sweet and the bitter. Sweet manioc roots may be cooked and eaten like a vegetable. Bitter manioc contains a poisonous acid, but the Indians learned long ago how to make a good food out of the roots by grinding them and pressing out the poisonous juice. This method is still used today. The pulp that remains can be shaped into little cakes and baked to make cassava bread. The Indians discovered further that the juice, if boiled down, loses its poison and makes an excellent sauce to flavor, tenderize, and preserve meats. In the United States it is used as a base for steak sauces.

How and when did the Indians discover the secret of bitter cassava and invent the grater and press for making good food out of it? No one knows, but they taught the Europeans how to prepare the roots, and their method has been followed ever since. The Spanish began eating cassava bread soon after they arrived in the Americas. Columbus stocked his ships with it as a substitute for ship's biscuit. Cassava bread keeps better than wheat biscuits; it is easy to prepare, and it tastes good. It was the main food of the first Spanish colonists in Mexico. The Portuguese took manioc to Africa, but it was not raised there in quantity until the twentieth century. Manioc and sweet potatoes are today probably the most important foods in the tropics throughout the world.

An interesting advantage of manioc is that it needs no storage. The roots can be left in the ground for as much as three or four years and dug up as needed. Have you ever eaten cassava? Possibly you have, but you gave it a different name. The only way people in the temperate zones see it is in the form of tapioca or sago, used in desserts.

Peanuts, also called ground nuts and goobers, may have been first cultivated in the Andes Mountains in Bolivia, but they were also raised in Mexico and Peru long before the Europeans arrived. The Spanish took this food to Africa in the 1500s, and slaves carried it to North America in the century that followed. In fact, *goober* is an African word for peanuts that the slaves brought into the English language. Peanuts were enjoyed by the colonists and have been popular in North America ever since.

Wherever peanuts are grown, they are considered a valuable food. Today this American Indian gift is important in fifty-five countries around the world. India raises the most, followed by China and Nigeria. Peanuts are part of Chinese agriculture, because they can be raised on land that is unsuitable for rice. The United States ranks fourth in world production, and goobers have been a major crop here since 1900. They are used as nuts, and their oil is important in the manufacture of various foods and of many nonfood products such as soap and plastics.

Did you know that our custom of chewing gum comes from the American Indians? Although chewing dried tree sap is a custom of many peoples of the world, some of the first may have been the Mayas, who used chicle, the milky juice of the tropical sapodilla tree. The Europeans learned from them to chew this gum. Although substitutes are sometimes used, chicle—tapped from wild trees in the jungles of Yucatán and Guatemala—makes the best gum.

The pineapple, which first grew either in Mexico or in tropical South America, is the principal fruit that the Indian people added to the world's diet, unless one counts the tomato as a fruit. The first pineapple taken to Spain was served to the king. A historian of the 1500s wrote of the event: "The most invincible King Ferdinand relates that he has eaten another fruit brought from those lands. It is like a pine-nut in color, covered with scales and firmer than a melon. Its flavor excels all other fruits. This fruit, which the King prefers to all others, does not grow on a tree, but upon a plant." After the Spanish learned from the Indians how to raise pineapples, they began to grow the fruit in Europe, where its popularity soon spread. Great quantities of pineapple are raised today, mostly in Hawaii.

Some food plants of the Americas grew wild; among them were nuts, rice, and berries. The first Americans gathered these foods but seldom bothered to raise them, because they grew in such abundance. No doubt the white men would have found these foods without help, but the Indians did teach them their use.

Wild rice was harvested but not cultivated by the Ojibwa and other peoples living in the Great Lakes region. It is still harvested in Minnesota, Wisconsin, and Manitoba today and is considered a rare treat.

The turkey is the only fowl of importance that the Indians domesticated. The bird was perhaps first raised in Mexico, but it was also valued by the Pueblo peoples of the American Southwest. In the 1500s Spaniards took turkeys to Europe, where they were raised for food. In the following century, English colonists brought tame birds back to North America, but they also shot wild turkeys in the forests along the coast. In recent times the turkey has become popular as a source of food in the United States the year round, not only at Thanksgiving. It is also enjoyed in many European countries.

Thus we see that the first Americans gave us an amazing number of foods which have become part of the world's food supply. It has been estimated that nearly half the world's food today consists of plants domesticated by the American

Indians. In the United States many Indian foods are regarded as national dishes. Can you imagine life without baked beans, corn on the cob, french fries, catsup, sweet potatoes, chili con carne, roast turkey, chocolate, vanilla, pumpkin pie, and pineapples—to mention only a few Indian foods? When we consider all these contributions of the Indians, we begin to realize what a profound effect the first Americans have had on our everyday lives.

CHAPTER
6

Corn—America's Main Crop

THE INDIANS' greatest contribution to world food is also by far the most important crop in the U. S. economy. This agricultural staple is corn, the third most valuable crop on earth, after wheat and rice. Corn is one of the world's most widely distributed plants. It is raised in regions all the way from Canada to southern Chile, and from Siberia to Africa. Corn can grow in soil that is too dry for rice and not dry enough for wheat and thus makes use of land that might otherwise be unused. In the United States corn is raised in each of the fifty states, although most of it is grown in the midwestern Corn Belt.

When Columbus came to America, corn was the leading crop in the Western Hemisphere, and it had been for more than two thousand years. As it is today, the crop was grown from what is now Canada to southern South America. French explorers found large stands of corn in the St. Lawrence Valley. Along the Ohio and Mississippi rivers cornfields stretched for miles. The Iroquois, an agricultural people, planted corn in what is now New York State. Corn was the main crop of the hardy Pueblo farmers of the Southwest. It was the major crop in Mexico. In Peru it was raised on the terraced mountainside farms of the Andes. It was an important product on both the Atlantic and Pacific coasts of South America. Among Indian peoples who lived mainly by hunting, the women took charge of the well-tended corn gardens. Among those who depended chiefly on agriculture, the men did the corn farming. In some cultures, men and women worked together in the cornfields.

The Indian peoples treasured corn as a gift from God. Many of their customs, traditions, myths, and industries and much of their religion and art centered on the sacred grain. Planting and harvesting were religious rituals. The so-called first Thanksgiving, celebrated at Plymouth in 1621, was a version of the harvest feast which the first Americans had held for centuries. Theirs was a religious ceremony in which the Indian people thanked God for giving them food to tide them through the winter.

Corn was the foundation of the three splendid Indian civilizations: the Maya and Aztec nations, both in Mexico, and the Inca empire in Peru. Those civilizations were made possible by their agriculture, of which corn was either the most important crop or, as in Peru, the second most important, after potatoes. Throughout the whole corn-raising region of the Americas the various peoples planted, cultivated, harvested, and prepared corn in much the same way.

The first white people who ever saw corn were two of Columbus's men exploring the interior of Cuba. They returned to the ships saying they had found a grain called "mah-eez" (maize), which was "well tasted, baked, dried, and made into flour." Whether Columbus took corn back to Europe is not known, but later explorers did. The Portuguese took it to Africa. Spanish ships took it to the countries around the Mediterranean. There Turkish traders may have bought sacks of the bright-colored seeds and taken them to the Orient, for early in the 1500s corn was being raised in China. Maize was adopted slowly in Europe, and it was long before it was raised there as a crop. Europeans who tasted the corn did not like it, but this may have been because no one had taught them how to prepare it properly. In England corn was known only as a curiosity to botanists until the early 1600s.

Most of the earliest English families who settled on the coasts of Virginia and Massachusetts had never seen corn, although they may have heard of it. But, as we saw in an earlier chapter, they soon learned what it was. We have also seen that the Pilgrims discovered corn even before they had found a place on the coast to establish their colony and before they had met any Indians. It was not only the first colonists who were saved when the Indians gave them the grain and taught them corn farming. Later settlers along the Ohio River, in the Mississippi Valley, and farther west also owed their lives to corn. As an Indian historian of the early 1900s expressed it: "The maize plant was the bridge over which English civilization crept, tremblingly and uncertainly at first, then boldly and surely, to a foothold and a permanent occupation of America."

The first colonists did not know what to call the yellow cereal. Some called it Indian wheat or Turkey wheat. Others called it Indian grain. But their word for grain was *corn,* as it still is in England, and so they called it Indian corn. Later they learned that one Indian name for it was *maize,* but by that time the word *corn* had come into general use. Today those who live in the United States, Canada, and Australia call the Indian grain corn, but the rest of the world more correctly calls it maize. When the word *corn* is used in the Bible and in other works written before 1492, it means grain, usually wheat.

In adopting corn as a crop, the white men did not take the seed and invent their own way of raising it. If they had plowed the ground and scattered seed corn over the field as they did wheat or oats, they would not have had a crop. The Indians had to teach them how to plant, cultivate, harvest, and store the grain and finally how to prepare it for eating. The Europeans' adoption of the Indian way of han-

These five cobs show the development of corn, or maize, between about 5000 B.C. and A.D. 1500. The oldest cob is less than an inch long. All come from excavations in the Tehuacán Valley, Mexico.
From Environment and Subsistence: The Prehistory of the Tehuacán Valley, Vol. 1, Douglas S. Byers, ed.

dling corn is well known and fully recorded. Only in recent times have white farmers made changes in the way they raise the grain. But even today, in the United States and in other lands, people still eat maize in the same ways that the first Americans prepared it long ago—as cornbread, corn on the cob, corn cereal, popcorn, Cracker Jacks, hominy, tortillas, tamales, and cornmeal mush.

What is this remarkable plant that was already so important in the Americas five hundred years ago and which has since then extended its influence over the whole earth? Where did it come from? Plant scientists have been exploring that mystery for many years. Corn is an annual grass, like wheat and oats. Those grains, native to the Eastern

Hemisphere, are still found there in the wild state. After thousands of years of cultivation, wheat has been improved as a crop, but it still looks much like wild wheat. Corn is different in that respect. The mystery is that no wild corn plant has ever been found.

In trying to understand better how to produce new varieties of corn, plant scientists have long searched for its wild ancestor. They have found ears of corn as well as pottery made in the shape of corn in ancient graves and ruins in both Mexico and South America. Although many of these findings are more than two thousand years old, the grain looks much like the corn of today. Botanists have examined many wild grasses in Mexico and Central America in their search for wild corn. Digging in caves in Mexico and in New Mexico where ancient peoples lived, archaeologists found tiny maize cobs. The deeper they dug, the smaller were the cobs they found, showing clearly how the corn plant developed through the centuries. The earliest cobs fitted the description of what an ancestor of corn might look like, but they clearly came from domesticated plants, even though they were believed to be more than four thousand years old. Later, tiny cobs only half an inch long were found in southern Mexico. They proved to be even older. Under a magnifying glass scientists could see that the cobs had tiny sockets that once held kernels, each enclosed in a pod. The plant on which they grew is believed by some scientists to be the forerunner of present-day maize. Other scientists believe that corn may have been developed from one or two wild grasses native to Mexico, but most agree that the American Indians began to cultivate corn possibly seven thousand years ago.

The ancestor of corn must have been a wild growth, totally unlike modern maize. That Indian farmers developed such a plant into one of the world's greatest cereals is almost impossible to believe. Only a plant scientist can truly appreciate what an achievement that was. It took skill, imagination, and a high degree of intelligence on the part of not one person, but generations of men and women who planted and harvested over thousands of years. The ear of corn has no equal anywhere in nature. The development of maize is "mankind's most remarkable plant-breeding achievement," according to George Beadle, an authority on the subject, in an article in the *Scientific American*.

The strangest feature of corn is that it is the most domesticated plant on earth. It is so highly domesticated that it cannot live and grow without human help. Nearly all domesticated plants have some trouble seeding themselves, but in this respect the corn plant is completely helpless. The present-day ear of maize is so tightly wrapped in its husks that if it falls to the ground all the kernels begin to sprout. None of the plants can mature, because the seeds rob one another of food and moisture, and thus all die. Corn can grow and mature only if separate kernels are planted and the plants are spaced and carefully tended.

Indian agriculturalists developed all the types of corn that are raised today: sweet corn, popcorn, and three kinds of field corn—dent, flour, and flint. Dent corn has a dent in the top of the kernel, because the hard and soft starches in it dry at different rates. Flour corn, which is mostly starch, is soft and easily ground. The starch in flint corn is hard, and the kernel is not dented. Popcorn is a kind of flint corn with a very hard kernel. The Indian people developed 150 varieties of corn to grow in many different climates. The Mandans, living in what is now North Dakota, developed corn that matured in sixty days. The Pueblo dwellers of the Southwest grew a variety that thrived in their hot, desert homeland. The people of Peru developed a kind that could grow without rain being watered only by dew.

The Indians developed maize by crossing different kinds or strains of corn. This is called making hybrids, or hybridization. When pollen from one kind of corn falls on the silk of another kind, the seed that results will be a new variety.

It will inherit some qualities from each parent plant. By such crossing, or crossbreeding, almost any kind of plant can be changed and improved. Although this was well known, the farmers of North America at first made little effort to improve the maize varieties they got from the Indians. Then, as one historian put it, "the white man rediscovered hybridization."

In 1877, nearly four hundred years after Columbus's voyages, plant scientists began to experiment with crossing corn varieties to produce a strain that would yield more bushels per acre. They had some success, and in the early 1900s they tried a new approach. Plants of certain strains were inbred; that is, each plant is fertilized with its own pollen. When the resulting inbred lines were crossed, it was found that some combinations resulted in vigorous plants that had unusually high yields. The new plants were then crossed with others to produce plants that would resist disease and drought, and mature early or late, as desired. When the seeds of this hybrid corn were sold, a farmer could buy just the kind he needed, to fit the climate, soil, and rainfall of the place where he lived. To produce the most dependable results, farmers used only seed that had been scientifically produced, instead of planting seeds from their last year's crop. This meant that companies were formed to raise seed corn. The fields of seed corn were located throughout corn-growing regions where the seed would later be used. Gradually farmers used more and more of the seed. In 1935 only 1 percent of the corn grown in the United States came from hybrid seed. By the 1960s nearly all corn was hybrid. By that time the seed corn business had grown to be so great that, in terms of dollars, it was bigger than the nation's steel industry. Companies raised seed for farmers in other countries as well.

It will come as no surprise that nearly half the world's corn is raised in the United States. The rest is grown in about eighty countries, of which Argentina, Mexico, and Russia raise the most. Although corn is used as food for both human beings and livestock, most of that grown in the United States is fed to pigs, cattle, and chickens. Thus most people here eat corn in the form of meat, eggs, and dairy products. Many, of course, also eat it in the form of sweet corn and other corn foods.

The corn that is not fed to livestock is made into human food and is used as a raw material in many kinds of manufactured goods, both food and nonfood products. That part of the corn crop is of great importance in our economy. Some of it can be easily recognized in grocery stores as sweet corn, popcorn, corn oil, corn cereal, corn syrup, and cornstarch. Corn is, however, used in making thousands of products in which it cannot be easily recognized.

In the last few decades chemical researchers have discovered that the corn kernel has an almost unlimited number of uses. The starch, sugar, and oil made from the kernel have proved useful in many ways. In one or more of these forms, maize enters the manufacture or preparation of so many foods that in today's supermarket almost all products except fresh fish, fruits, and vegetables depend on this Indian gift in some way.

Cornstarch keeps ingredients from separating in such foods as candies, baked goods, salad dressings, canned soups, and various desserts. It is an important ingredient in powdered sugar and baking powder. The nonfood uses of cornstarch are many times greater than the food uses. For example, the starch is important for its binding quality in making cloth, paper, matches, packaging, inks, upholstery products, paint, furniture, television tubes, medicines, linoleum, detergents, oilcloth, adhesive tape, toys, crayons, chalk, plastics, tires, machine parts, road surfacing, wallboard, dynamite, and many, many more products.

More than half the cornstarch that is manufactured is converted into corn syrup and corn sugar, or dextrose. In these forms, its food uses are greater than its nonfood uses.

If you think corn syrup is just like other sweeteners, you are mistaken. Corn syrup has some characteristics that make it especially valuable. Unlike ordinary white or brown sugar, it will not crystallize. It also keeps other sugars from crystallizing. That is why a fudge recipe may call for corn syrup in addition to other sugars. Candy manufacturers put corn syrup into almost every kind of candy. Corn syrup, added to ice cream, keeps ice crystals from forming. Another special characteristic of corn syrup is that it stabilizes moisture. Products containing it, such as tobacco or cosmetics, will neither dry out nor get soggy.

Corn sugar, or dextrose, is used in the manufacture of many foods and in other ways as well. Chewing gum manufacturers, for instance, have discovered that it is the only sweetener that will hold the flavor in gum. In a caramelized form, it makes an excellent coloring for cold drinks, medicines, and candies. Doctors have also found an important use for dextrose in hospitals. Since dextrose is the same as the sugar in human blood, it acts as a predigested food. For that reason it can be used to put nourishment directly into the veins of patients who have had surgery, have been severely injured, or are unable to eat normally for some other reason. Such intravenous (into the veins) feeding saves many lives every day.

Corn oil also finds its way into both food and nonfood products. As a shortening, it is used in bakery goods, salad dressings, and almost any other food that contains grease in some form. Nonfood uses include the making of soap, cosmetics, some ammunitions, rubber substitutes, and such items as rust-preventive compounds.

Besides the grain kernel, other parts of the corn plant are also useful. The leaves and stalks are cut up for animal feed. Paper and wallboard can be made out of the stalks. Cobs have long been used as fuel, and some are made into tobacco pipes. Finely ground corncobs make an excellent material to clean and polish jewelry, machine parts, and other metal objects. The cobs also contain a chemical that can be added to oil to keep automobile engines running smoothly.

Although the corn kernel developed by the Indians has such a wealth of useful elements, it is less than perfect in one way: it is not a complete food—like milk, for instance. Corn is rich in carbohydrate or starch and also contains oil and some protein. But the protein in corn is not complete or balanced. It lacks two elements that the body needs for health and growth. The more important of these is lysine (lye SEEN). In the early 1960s, plant scientists accidentally found a way to change this. Their achievement is of special importance because there are so many hungry people on earth today. At present the human race desperately needs a kind of food that can be produced easily and cheaply and has all the food elements that the body needs.

Crossing several kinds of corn, scientists in one university laboratory produced maize plants with kernels that were opaque (o PAKE); that is, light did not shine through them as it does through kernels of ordinary corn. When they tested kernels of these strains, they discovered that one of them, which they called Opaque-2, had twice as much lysine as normal corn. In fact, it was as rich in balanced protein as milk, and nearly as rich as meat. This was electrifying news. If a supercorn could be produced that was rich in both carbohydrate and protein, it could save millions of starving people. The scientists planted some of the dull kernels. After several seasons of planting, enough new corn had been grown so that it could be tested as feed for livestock. The results were a great success. Now scientists knew that Opaque-2 is a complete food. Then came a more important test. The corn was prepared as food and eaten by humans. Undernourished children who had nothing else to eat were normal and healthy after three months.

The agriculturalists then still had an enormous job to perform. They had to cross this corn with other strains to produce a grain that would not only have a high quality protein but would also resist drought and disease, produce a high yield per acre, and grow in the climates and soils of the many nations where corn is a major crop. Such a task would take far more scientists and field test plots than any agricultural school could possibly have. This was a worldwide project. In 1970 the United Nations chose an international crop improvement center in Mexico to undertake the giant task of producing the needed seed grain. The work was paid for by funds from the United Nations, private foundations, international agencies, and the governments of nearly two dozen nations. Besides those who worked on the project in Mexico, scientists in nearly fifty countries around the world also helped. Seeds from every crossbreeding have had to be field tested, or grown, in every country where the corn would later be used. This meant raising and testing millions of plants. As the project is completed, seed becomes available for every climate and soil condition where it is to be grown. Then farmers in all those regions can raise a grain that is a complete food. The new high-lysine corn truly fulfills the meaning of the Indian word *maize*—"that which sustains life."

In the late 1970s plant scientists, searching in the mountains of Mexico, found a rare form of the wild grass called teocinte (tee o SIN te), a distant relative of corn. This variety of the plant, which can be crossbred with corn, is a perennial; that is, it grows up each year from its roots and does not need to be replanted. Although the project might take ten years, botanists believe that, by crossbreeding the two plants, they can produce perennial corn. Since much of the cost of growing grain goes into plowing under the old crop and sowing the new, this new plant would eliminate much of the cost of corn farming. In fact, it would revolutionize the raising of corn and make it even more valuable than before. Crossing maize with the hardy teocinte would also result in a plant that is more resistant to disease than present-day corn. But the new crop would still be the same maize that the first Americans domesticated centuries ago. This contribution from the Indians is perhaps the greatest gift of any people to mankind.

CHAPTER
7

Potatoes—The Vegetable That Changed History

OF THE many food plants the world learned about from the American Indians, the potato is the one that perhaps half the people on earth eat every day. It was the farmers of ancient Peru and nearby regions of the Andes who developed this vegetable from its wild state. After potatoes were first seen by Europeans in the 1500s, nearly two hundred years passed before people of the Eastern Hemisphere would accept the Peruvian vegetable, but when they finally did, potatoes became one of the earth's leading foods. Potatoes produce more nourishment per acre than corn and more than twice as much as wheat and rice. The value of this vegetable to the human race is so great that it can hardly be calculated. Few foods have affected history as much.

The potato belongs to a large plant family that includes the tomato, the sweet and chili pepper, and the poisonous nightshade. Potatoes are easy to raise: they like cool weather and sandy soil, but they will also grow in other climates and soils. The part of the plant that we eat is a tuber—the thickened end of an underground stem. The potato is most valued for its starch, but it also contains vitamin C, one of the B vitamins, a small amount of protein, and several important minerals.

Potatoes were the leading crop in the central Andes Mountains when the first Europeans arrived there in the early 1500s. They are still raised in the Peruvian highlands and are still the main food of the people who live there. The potato was already domesticated four thousand years ago. Pieces of the vegetable, in remarkably good condition, have been found in ancient garbage heaps in the desert along the Pacific coast of South America. Vases shaped like potatoes, along with the dried tubers, have been found in tombs along the same coast. These findings tell us that the people of the Andes were eating potatoes long, long ago.

The first European to see potatoes, at least the first one to leave a record, was the Spanish historian Pedro de Cieza de León who came across them in what is now Colombia in the early 1500s. His account describes the potatoes—which the Incas called *papas*—as "a kind of ground nut, which when boiled become as soft as a cooked chestnut." The crop was valuable in the mountainous regions, because it can be grown at altitudes that are too high and too cold for corn and most other plants.

The Spanish missionary José de Acosta told of seeing the *papas* so valued by the Andean people, in the 1570s: "*Papas* are eaten boiled or roasted. Indeed, these roots are the only wealth of the land, and when the season is favorable for the crop, the Indians are glad." Acosta and other early historians describe how the Indians froze and dried the *papas* so that "they will remain unspoiled for years." This was no doubt the world's first freeze-dried food. People living in the Andean highlands today preserve their crop in the same way.

In 1578 Sir Francis Drake, the English navigator, came across potatoes in Chile. At about the same time, Spanish authorities were beginning to raise them in Peru to feed the sailors on their ships. No one knows when potatoes were first taken to Europe, but possibly the Spaniards took them there in the late 1500s. Accounts written by Cieza, Acosta, and others aroused the interest of European botanists of the time, who were curious about all plants brought from the strange, faraway Americas.

Although such Indian crops as beans, peppers, and tobacco were becoming popular in Europe and other parts of the world by the 1600s, it took another century before the humble, harmless potato was recognized as the nourishing food that it is. Meanwhile the plant was raised in gardens in England and on the European continent where people looked on it as a curiosity or raised it for its flowers.

The poor peasants of Ireland seem to have been the first people in the Eastern Hemisphere to plant potatoes as a crop and to eat them regularly. Whenever they may have arrived, we know that potatoes were being raised there by the mid-1600s. The sandy soil and cool climate of the island made the crop so successful that the Irish peasants eventually ate almost nothing but potatoes—morning, noon, and night. This Indian vegetable yielded such a generous harvest that a family who would have starved on four acres of wheat had plenty to eat if they planted less than two acres in potatoes. Besides, grain had to be ground, made into bread, and baked before it could be eaten, while potatoes had only to be roasted in the fire or boiled.

Outside Ireland, potatoes did not find such favor. The prejudice of the common people arose from their belief that the plant was harmful. Was the potato not related to the deadly nightshade? Potatoes were not cultivated in France until the late 1700s. At about the same time, they were taken to Norway, Sweden, and Russia, and their use increased in Scotland. Although some potatoes may have been brought to North America somewhat earlier, we know they reached the American colonies in 1719 when Scotch-Irish families brought them to New Hampshire. Their New England neighbors, even when they saw the success of the crop, did not grow it in their own fields for a long time.

Gradually the popularity of the potato spread, both in the United States and in Europe, and gradually people began to consider it a necessity of life. Since the tuber from Peru was feeding hungry millions in so many countries, some economists and government leaders believed that a food had been found that would wipe out famine for all time. Yet strangely enough, this very potato caused one of the worst famines in history. The Irish, as we said, depended on this crop for nearly all their food. But if farmers raise only one crop, and that crop fails, the people have nothing to eat. That is what happened in Ireland. In the early 1840s, a blight or mildew that had always killed a few plants spread through the potato fields of Europe and America and destroyed nearly all the plants. In lands where potatoes were only one of several foods, there might have been hunger, but in Ireland, with only one crop, there was starvation. By the end of the 1840s, one million people had died. Another million, as a result of the famine, migrated to America.

Was the potato then abandoned as a crop to feed the hungry? Not at all. As has happened before, disaster brought about improvement. The potato blight in Ireland led to the development of plant pathology, the science that studies plant diseases and tries to find cures. Pathologists learned that such plant conditions are caused by tiny organisms. In the case of the potato blight, locating the cause made it possible to find a remedy—a spray that would kill the offending mold. This discovery led to the control of other plant diseases—all because of the potato.

The potato famine and the widespread use of potatoes in many lands also led to the development of new varieties of the plant. After 1850 botanists began to develop potatoes that would grow in various climates and kinds of soil, that would mature early or late in the season, and that would resist drought, frost, and diseases.

By the 1900s this American Indian vegetable was being raised in most countries where weather and soil are favorable. Germany was raising a third of the world crop, Russia nearly a quarter. During the first and second world wars the

Germans were kept alive by the potatoes they could raise. Many people in Poland and France survived only because of their potato crops.

In 1910 more pounds of this Indian vegetable were raised than of any other food crop on earth. By midcentury the world total was more than eight billion bushels a year. This meant that potatoes ranked with wheat, rice, and corn as one of the main food crops of the world. Among vegetables, the potato leads all others. As a food for either human beings or livestock, it is the cheapest and best source of carbohydrate or starch.

In 1973 potatoes were raised in nearly every country, but they were especially important in the lands of northern Europe. Potatoes are also an important crop in most other European countries and in nearly every land in North and South America. Their value is increased by the fact that this Indian plant will produce a good harvest on poor land where almost nothing else will grow.

The most valued potato product is starch. It goes into the making of glue, paper, textiles, alcohol, and various foods. In Russia large amounts of potatoes are used in making vodka, the famous Russian liquor.

By 1970s potatoes were providing 25 percent of the world's food while taking up only 5 percent of its cropland. The vegetable could, however, still be raised successfully only in cool climates. In 1972, in an attempt to overcome this disadvantage, several international government agencies cooperated in opening a potato-improvement center in Lima, Peru. There, researchers have succeeded in creating a fast-growing potato that will thrive in the hot, humid tropics. When this variety of the plant has been crossbred to have resistance to disease and other desirable qualities, the lowly potato will be more valuable than ever.

CHAPTER
8
Rubber—Wonder Substance

THE MOST unusual plant material the world learned about from the Indian people is rubber. Rubber is used to make products such as tires for automobiles, trucks, and airplanes; small objects like erasers and rubber bands; footballs, basketballs, tennis shoes, and other sports items; rainwear; and thousands of medical and industrial products, most of them unfamiliar to the average person. The manufacture of rubber goods is one of the great industries of the twentieth century. Modern civilization could not have developed without it.

Rubber is a solid, made from a milky liquid called latex (LAY tex) found in the stems and roots of certain plants that grow in hot, humid regions. When a rubber plant is cut or scratched, the latex oozes out. After the air touches it, the liquid slowly hardens into the solid material we call rubber. Rubber has many unusual qualities. It is tough; it is unbreakable; air, water, and electricity cannot go through it. When it is soft it can be molded into any shape. Its most unusual and important characteristic is that it is elastic, stretchy. If rubber is pulled or squeezed, it will spring back as soon as it is released. Some kinds can be stretched to ten times their length. In all nature there is no other substance like rubber.

Latex-producing plants grow in Africa and Asia as well as in the Americas. Yet it was the Indians of Mexico and Central and South America who had the imagination and creative genius to make rubber, discover its properties, and find uses for the material.

The first Europeans to see rubber were Columbus and his men on the admiral's second voyage to the New World. One Spanish historian tells us that Columbus saw people in Haiti playing a game with balls "made of the gum of a tree" which "though heavy, would fly and bound" and looked "as if they had been alive." Another writer described how the explorer Cortes and his soldiers, in 1519, watched teams of Aztecs playing a game of ball on a big public court in Mexico. He says that they played with big balls "made from the juice of a certain herb." The juice was hardened by heat and "when struck on the ground but softly, would rebound incredibly into the air."

It is hard to believe that neither Columbus nor Cortes saw what a wonderful substance the strange material was. Neither explorer said anything about rubber in his accounts or letters. We learn of it from the records of men who were with them. Some historians say that Columbus and Cortes, or their men, took samples of rubber back to Europe. If they did, no one there apparently took any interest in it. And little mention of rubber was made in writings during the century that followed. Yet during that time there were many Spanish and Portuguese soldiers, priests, and government officials in those parts of the Americas where rubber was being made.

A Spanish historian writing in 1615 mentioned the "magical tree gum" as being used for something other than sport. He told how Indians of Mexico gathered the milky juice from cuts made in tree trunks and brushed them on cloaks to make them waterproof. They also spread it on their feet, layer after layer, to make rubber shoes. Long experiment had taught them that if they dried each layer in hot smoke before adding another layer, the rubber was stronger and more durable.

During the 1800s archaeologists uncovered the ruins of many of the ball courts of which the early Spanish historians had written. Near one of them in Mexico they found a sacred well into which rubber balls had been dropped. Excavations in Central and South America have shown that Indians were using rubber in those regions more than a thousand years ago.

After the report that was written in 1615, another century was to pass before Europeans found out more about rubber, and then it was rather by accident. In the 1730s the Paris Academy of Sciences sent an expedition to South America to take measurements of the earth at the equator. One man in the group was the geographer Charles de la Condamine. While traveling in the Amazon Valley, he saw people making and using rubber and decided to find out more about it. He became the first European to study the properties of the substance, and he wrote the first serious account of how it was made and used. In the jungles of Brazil he saw Indians use rubber to waterproof their clothes and to make rubber shoes, hollow balls, and breast plates. They would make a hollow object, like a syringe, by dipping a mold of clay into latex again and again until a thick layer formed. When the rubber had hardened, they would strike the object against a rock to crumble the mold, which they would wash out through a little hole, leaving the hollow rubber piece.

La Condamine wrote of rubber: "When it is fresh, they work it with molds into any shape they please. Rain does not go through it. But what makes it most remarkable is its elasticity. They make bottles of it, which are not easy to break; boots and hollow bowls which may be squeezed flat, and when no longer squeezed, spring back to their first shape." When La Condamine saw Indians in Brazil make quivers for their arrows, he decided that rubber would be a fine material out of which to make cases to protect his scientific instruments against the jungle damp. This is the first time that a European recognized the value of what the Indians had been doing for hundreds of years.

After La Condamine presented an account of his discoveries to the Paris Academy, scientists at last began to take an interest in rubber, and samples were sent or brought from the Americas. One sample came into the hands of the English scientist Joseph Priestly, the man who discovered oxygen. When he found that it would erase pencil marks if rubbed over paper, he called the material *rubber*. And since he knew that some of it came from the West Indies, he named it India rubber. It was called that for more than a century, leading many people to believe that the material came from India.

By the time rubber began to be used widely in Europe and the United States, botanists had found that the most important latex plant was the hevea (HEE ve a) tree, which grows along the Amazon River in Brazil. In fact it is the only rubber plant worth raising commercially. In the late 1800s English botanists took seeds of this tree to Southeast Asia, where the climate is hot and humid but cultivation is easier than in the jungles of South America. There large plantations were started, where rubber could be grown commercially. These plantations proved to be highly successful. In the 1980s more than eleven million acres of rubber trees grew in Malaya, Indonesia, and Africa.

Through the years, the world found more and more uses for this American Indian product. The invention of the automobile, the spread in the use of electricity, the development of the science of medicine, the growth of sports—all increased the need for rubber. Even in our most modern uses of the substance, however, we are still following many practices invented by Indians before Columbus. We make molded products such as rubber gloves by dipping forms into liquid rubber and adding layer after layer. We make rubberized coats and boots to keep dry in the rain, as they

did. And we have certainly copied the Indians in making rubber balls for sports. Even today, the manufacture of rubber balls is a difficult process—whether complicated golf balls or simple play balls for children. This shows the skill that the Indians must have had to make the large, heavy balls that Columbus and Cortes saw them playing with five hundred years ago. One observer in the Amazon region saw Indians mix sulphur with rubber and heat the mixture to get a better product. This, of course, is vulcanizing, which the Indians discovered long before Charles Goodyear rediscovered it in the 1830s.

As early as 1825 some chemists began to examine rubber in the laboratory to find out how nature put it together and to try to make artificial rubber. By the 1960s several kinds of synthetic rubber were being made. But for some important uses, such as tires for automobiles, buses, trucks, and airplanes, natural rubber is still needed. In fact, one-third of the rubber used today is the natural product, and the amount is increasing.

Since synthetic rubber is made from petrochemicals, which are growing more scarce and costly, it is expected that natural rubber will be more and more in demand in the future. Companies that use large amounts of rubber are trying to meet this demand by expanding their rubber plantations around the world.

Although rubber is used worldwide, few people today know that we owe this amazing product to the genius of the American Indians.

Indian people in the South American jungles learned to make rubber more than a thousand years ago out of latex, the juice of the hevea tree. The modern-day Brazilian shown here is tapping a tree much as inhabitants of the area did long ago.

Goodyear Rubber Company

CHAPTER
9
Medicines and Medical Practices Adopted from the First Americans

As WE have seen, the first Europeans in the Western Hemisphere began to depend on the Indian people as soon as they landed. Besides helping them in other ways, the Indians sometimes cured their ailments and injuries. The medical help that the whites received in the Americas during the 1500s and 1600s and even later was often better than the treatment they would have received in Europe, where doctors were still treating diseases by prescribing mummy dust and powdered bats' eyes.

One of the earliest reported cures of white men by Indians took place in 1535. When the French explorer Jacques Cartier was on his second voyage to North America, his ships froze fast in the St. Lawrence River, and many of his men became ill with scurvy, a sickness much feared by seafaring men. Twenty-five died, and the rest were desperately sick.

The Indian people sometimes suffered from scurvy in winter, but they knew how to cure it. One day Cartier met a group of Indian men among whom was one who had been very sick with the disease only ten days earlier. The Frenchman was amazed to see that he was "whole and sound," as the report says. Cartier asked how the man had recovered and was told that he "had taken the juice and sap of the leaves of a certain tree." The Indians generously got some of the bark and needles of an evergreen and showed the explorer how to make a medicine by boiling them. Cartier's sailors at first hesitated to take the strange medicine, but when they did so they were cured. This is only one of dozens of cases on record in which American Indians cured explorers, traders, soldiers, and others of the disease.

Scurvy had been known in the Old World since ancient times. Medical men ascribed it to many causes, but no one realized that the only people who got the illness were those who had been deprived of certain foods. We know now that scurvy is a deficiency disease caused by a lack of vitamin C, which is found especially in various fresh plants. The first Americans knew that in winter, when there were no other green plants in the northern regions, the bark and needles of several evergreens, as well as various herbs, contained a cure for the disease.

Two centuries after Cartier's experience, the Scottish naval physician James Lind read of the incident. This information gave him the idea for experiments that led him to find the cause of scurvy. Although the preventive would no doubt have been discovered eventually, the Native Americans must be given credit for helping to uncover the cause of this illness that plagued mankind for so long.

After the explorers and traders came the frontiersmen and colonists. They also learned to value medicines offered them by the Indian, since there were few medical doctors among them. Gradually Indian drugs and herbs became folk medicines—the home remedies that pioneer families depended on. In time these remedies came to the attention of medical men, first the saddlebag doctors of the frontier, then the more highly educated physicians. When medical doctors tried the medicines, they found that some produced uncertain results, others were useful, and a few were of great value. As various

Indian remedies were seen to be helpful, they were placed on the lists of official drugs published by medical authorities in *The Pharmacopoeia of the United States of America (USP)*, which began publication in 1820, and the *National Formulary (NF)*, first published in 1888. In the course of time more than two hundred Indian drugs were incorporated into these two books. Indian medicines were taken up in similar books in Europe.

During the last century many natural plant remedies listed in the *USP* and *NF* were replaced by synthetic drugs developed by laboratory scientists. Although most Indian medicines have been replaced by such compounds, we must remember that they provided models for the man-made substitutes we use today. A few plant medicines of the American Indians, however, have not been replaced by products of even the most advanced chemistry. Among them are some that are used throughout the world.

Several important Indian medical discoveries came from South America. It is from there that the world first heard of quinine, which has been called one of our most valuable medicines. As the treatment for malaria, this drug has saved the lives of millions of people. Malaria, a serious infectious disease carried from one person to another by mosquitoes, is one of the earth's most ancient plagues; it is said to have taken more lives than all the wars in history. People formerly believed that the sickness was caused by bad air, because it often occurs near swamps, where mosquitoes breed. In fact, the word *malaria* comes from two Italian words meaning "bad air." The disease is found in all warm regions and is especially widespread in India, where there are still millions of cases each year.

The medicine we call quinine was the first successful treatment for malaria, and between the early 1600s and the early 1900s, it was the only one. Where did it come from?

Quinine is made from the bark of the cinchona (sin KO na) tree, which grows wild in the jungles in the Andes Mountains. The earliest reliable account of the use of cinchona bark is dated 1600, when a priest in Peru is reported to have been cured of a fever by bark that was given to him by an Indian. The Spanish mayor of a Peruvian city was cured some years later. Cinchona was mentioned in a report by a Spanish missionary priest in Peru in 1630s who wrote: "A tree grows which they call the fever tree . . . whose bark cures the fevers. . . . It has produced miraculous results in Lima [Peru]." The author does not give the Indians, among whom he labored, credit for finding the tree, but many Spanish invaders credited the Indian people very little for the treasures they got from them. Although news of the healing bark reached the Spanish in Peru through the missionaries, there is no evidence that the priests discovered it.

The healing bark was taken to Europe by a Spanish viceroy of Peru, the Count of Chinchon. His name, misspelled, was later given to the tree. For the next hundred years, cinchona bark was used in Europe for various ailments. Its use continued and spread, even though Europeans knew little about the tree from which it came.

By the mid-1800s both the English and the Dutch were importing the bark. But they feared that the supply would not last, because the number of trees was dwindling. For that reason they decided to take cinchona seeds and small trees to their colonies in the East Indies, where they thought the tree should grow as well as in the Andes. This had to be done carefully, for Peru and Bolivia wanted to keep the rare plant, which at that time grew nowhere else in the world. England and Holland sent plant scientists to the Andes at various times in the 1800s, both secretly and openly, to bring back seeds and small trees. Every venture failed. Even when some trees were successfully raised, it was found that they were the wrong kind, with bark that had little quinine. After spending years of labor and several fortunes, it became clear that the European experts knew little about the fever-bark tree.

Finally Charles Ledger, an English bark dealer, succeeded in getting seeds of the cinchona tree with the highest yielding bark, which were then planted in the East Indies. But he did so only with the help—and the sacrifice—of an Indian from Bolivia. Ledger lived in Peru in the mid-1800s and, with a Bolivian servant named Manuel Mamani, had spent years tramping through the mountains examining cinchona trees and deciding which ones to buy for their bark. Mamani had an unusual knowledge of cinchona trees. He showed Ledger twenty-nine different kinds, when the best botanists in Europe knew of only nineteen. Mamani also knew which kind contained the most quinine, but in spite of their searches, he and the Englishman never found that kind.

One day Ledger asked his companion, "Do you think we will ever find the 'true' bark?" He meant the kind of tree with the most quinine. To this, Mamani answered confidently, "No, señor. The trees hereabouts do not see the snow-capped mountains." This was the Indian man's way of saying that the "true" bark tree grows only in areas that are within sight of high peaks of the Andes. Clearly he knew where such trees grew.

After many years Mamani returned to his native Bolivia where he again hired out as a bark collector. During his fourth winter there, he made a dangerous journey, traveling 800 miles on foot across the Andes, back to Peru where he had left Ledger. With him he carried a package of seeds of the kind of cinchona tree that yields the highest percentage of pure quinine. Only a person with skill and knowledge could have found the place in the jungle where they grew. After delivering the package, Mamani had to hurry back across the mountains before the opening of the bark-cutting season, when his fellow workers would notice his absence. But his absence was noted. Mamani reached home safely only to be condemned to death for betraying his people by giving a foreigner some of the nation's treasure.

Manuel Mamani received no credit for his sacrifice, but he

did accomplish his purpose. The seeds he gave to Ledger (there are 98,000 in an ounce) were taken, some to India, some to Java. Those planted in India died. But those in Java, skillfully nurtured by Dutch planters and scientists, lived and grew, resulting in large plantations of the trees, now called *Cinchona ledgeriana.* Tests proved that the bark had a quinine content of 13 percent, instead of the 2 or 3 percent found in other varieties. This was indeed the true bark.

Quinine remained the only treatment for malaria until the 1930s, when German scientists discovered how to make a synthetic compound to treat the disease. During World War II the Allies could not get this drug. At the same time, the quinine made in Holland from Javanese bark fell into German hands, and armed forces of Japan captured the cinchona plantations in Java. Then, when the armies of the United States went into North Africa and the South Pacific, two big malaria regions of the world, they had no dependable source of medicine to fight the disease. During the first campaign in the Philippines, when eighty-five of every hundred United States soldiers there contracted malaria, medicine became as important as military weapons. To deal with the problem, new synthetic drugs were developed in the United States, and men were sent to gather bark from wild cinchona trees in South America. During the 1960s in Vietnam, quinine again played an important role. Some strains of malaria there were not affected by man-made drugs, but natural quinine, used with other medicines, treated the disease successfully. In India and other tropical areas man-made drugs usually are not available, and quinine is still the main remedy for malaria. In the United States, where malaria is rare, the disease is treated with synthetic drugs, and quinine is used for other ailments such as muscle cramps. Quinidine (KWIN i deen), made from cinchona bark, is important in the treatment of certain heart diseases.

After more than a century, most cinchona still comes from Java. The bark is sent to Holland, where 90 percent of the world's quinine is produced. Some cinchona trees are cultivated in the Andes Mountains, and some wild trees there are cut for their bark.

An old and strange habit of the Incas brought about the discovery of the world's first local anesthetic. Long ago, people living in the Andes discovered that chewing the leaves of a certain plant that grew in the mountain jungles would take away hunger, tiredness, and other discomforts. The leaves they chewed were those of the coca (KO ca) plant. This shrub, native to the eastern slopes of the Andes and nowhere else, was known and used by the people of the region for centuries. Bags of the leaves have been found in graves in Peru that are more than a thousand years old. Coca was the "divine" plant of the Incas, highly valued by their physicians for its power to take away pain. It was also burned as incense in religious ceremonies and widely used as an item of trade.

The Spanish invaders observed the chewing habit of the Incas and soon learned the magical power of the leaves. In time, European botanists examined the plant, but for three centuries they found no practical use for it. In the mid-1800s two German chemists at last extracted the element in the plant that holds its strange power. They called it cocaine (ko CANE). Scientists wondered how the substance might be used, since it did not cure any disease.

In the 1860s a doctor experimenting with solutions of cocaine, placed a drop on the tip of his tongue. He noticed that the spot became numb, but after a short time feeling returned. Experimenting with animals, he found that cocaine seemed to take away feeling in the eyes of frogs and guinea pigs. Hearing of this, Carl Koller, a young doctor in Vienna, Austria, decided that perhaps cocaine could be used as a local anesthetic during surgical operations. A local anesthetic, which would take away feeling in part of the body, did not then exist. After more experiments Dr. Koller was at last ready to test his idea. He put a few drops of cocaine into the eye of a patient and then operated. The patient felt no pain. His success soon led physicians and dentists in many lands to start using the drug as an anesthetic.

Because it was found that cocaine had certain undesirable side effects, it was necessary to look for a local anesthetic that had the good characteristics of cocaine but not the bad. To supply this need, scientists created drugs patterned after the natural plant product. The first compound was procaine, better known as novocaine. It is still used by some physicians and dentists, although other substitutes have been developed.

Man-made compounds have almost completely taken the place of the natural product, but cocaine still has important uses in medicine. Forms of cocaine are listed in both the *USP* and the *NF*.

Today the descendants of the ancient Incas still chew coca leaves to help them endure cold weather, muscle strain, and other discomforts. Their coca-leaf chewing is neither harmful nor dangerous, for little cocaine is obtained in this way. Pure cocaine, however, extracted from the leaves by manufacture, is a powerful drug that is very dangerous if misused. Those who are foolish enough to use it as a stimulant will find that it is habit forming and seriously affects the nervous system. For this reason, the sale and use of cocaine are strictly controlled by law.

Another powerful drug first made in the jungles of South America is curare (kyoo RAH ri). This substance is a poison, yet it is useful in the practice of medicine, and various forms of the drug have been listed in the *USP* since 1916. Indian people along the Amazon learned to made curare out of native plants. They applied the drug to the tips of arrows to kill enemies and wild animals.

In the early 1500s the Spanish in South America noticed that an animal shot with a curare-tipped arrow became limp and stopped breathing almost at once, even though it had only a small wound. This made the Spaniards wonder what curare was and how it was made. Although the poison was used throughout a wide area by different peoples, nowhere could the white men find answers to their questions. In each tribe the secret was known to only a few leaders, who would not reveal it.

Curare continued to be a mystery for nearly three centuries. Not until the early 1800s did botanists and other scientists, exploring along the Amazon, find out from the people there which plants were used to make the poison. In 1844 a French chemist demonstrated that if curare is put into a muscle, that muscle becomes limp and cannot be moved. When the muscles of breathing cannot be moved or controlled, death results from lack of oxygen. That explains why men and animals died quickly when shot by poisoned arrows.

Even after these discoveries, another century passed before scientists could get enough curare for further study. Then experiments showed that, since curare relaxes muscles, it can be used to treat ailments in which tense, rigid muscles are a problem. Its first successful use was in 1942. Since then several man-made substitutes have been created that have the same effect as curare but are less dangerous to use. Doctors, however, still prescribe curare to relax muscles in certain abnormal conditions.

Cascara sagrada (Spanish for "holy bark") is a laxative made from the bark of a tree that grows on the West Coast of North America. Tradition says that a Spanish priest found Indian people there using the bark more than two centuries ago. Like so many other Indian remedies, it was adopted by the white people and widely used. In the late 1800s it was officially approved by the medical profession. Cascara sagrada, usually called simply cascara, was listed in the USP in 1890 and has been there ever since. It has been called the most widely used laxative on earth. The best sources of this medicine are certain bucktorn trees that grow in Washington, Oregon, upper California, and British Columbia. Since cascara cannot be made artificially, its place in the *USP* may be permanent.

People of Brazil discovered that ipecac (IP i kak), a medicine made from the roots of a jungle tree, is helpful in treating an intestinal illness called amoebic dysentery (a ME bik DIS en tarry). The Spanish began using it about 1600, and it has long been recognized by the medical profession. The shrub from which ipecac is made has been transplanted to India and Malaya where it is widely raised to provide the medicine. In the United States ipecac has been largely replaced by synthetic drugs in the treatment of dysentery. One form of ipecac, however, is of great value in treating patients who have swallowed poison. Doctors also find it useful in treating some other ailments. Ipecac has been listed in the *USP* since the book began publication in 1820.

Several Indian medicines have proved of value in healing wounds, sores, and other skin conditions. Among them are balsam of Peru and balsam of Tolu, the latter a drug from Colombia. Seneca Indians taught the New England colonists that a thick form of petroleum was a healing ointment for wounds and sores. It is used today in a slightly different and purified form that we know as petroleum jelly, with the most commonly used brand being Vaseline. Witch hazel and oil of wintergreen were discovered by the first Americans to be soothing relief for sore joints and muscles. Boneset, listed in the *USP* for nearly a century, was long used to control fevers. During the Civil War doctors used it to treat the colds and fevers of soldiers on both sides of the conflict. Doctors also considered dogwood root useful to treat "fever and ague." The root of the mayapple plant was valued as a gentle laxative and for its other properties. It is still found in the *USP*. Pinkroot, sassafras, and elm bark were Indian remedies kept in the home of the pioneer family and in the little black bag of the country doctor. Although most have been replaced by man-made compounds, they were long useful.

The plant remedies described in this chapter are only a

few of the natural medicines used by the Indian people. Those mentioned here are the main ones that the rest of the world adopted and has benefited from.

The first Americans invented a device used every day in medical practice—the bulbed syringe. Some tribes made the syringe out of an animal bladder, with a hollow bone or reed stuck into the opening. The Ojibwa of the Great Lakes region used that kind. Indian people living along the Amazon, where rubber trees grow, made syringes out of rubber, an idea that the white men copied. Early traders and explorers saw the syringe being used as far north as Canada and southward to the Amazon. Its use is shown in the decorations on ancient pottery and mentioned in an Aztec manuscript dated 1552. Present-day syringes do not differ in principle or use from those invented by the Indian people.

Finally we must mention the guinea pig, which the Andes people contributed to present-day medical research. They raised the animal for meat, but in modern science it has proved of great value in testing drugs and medical procedures.

CHAPTER
10
Tobacco—The Strange and Pleasant Weed

NOT LONG after Columbus reached North America, he came across an Indian who "had some dried leaves, which must be a thing highly prized by them because they barter in it." Some time later, he sent two men ashore on an island off the coast to explore the interior. They returned and told him they had met "men and women with a half-burnt weed in their hands, which is the herb they are accustomed to smoke." The weed, of course, was tobacco. These were the first of countless occasions when the first European explorers found Indian people using tobacco in both Americas.

The newcomers did not always agree about the Indian custom. A Portuguese discoverer in Brazil reported that he took up smoking and added, "I found it refreshing." Jacques Cartier, exploring in Canada in the early 1500s, had a different reaction. He wrote that the Indian people had a plant which "they hold in high esteem. . . . After drying it in the sun they carry it around their necks in a small skin pouch, together with a hollow bit of stone or wood. At frequent intervals they crumble this plant into powder which they place in one of the openings of the hollow instrument and, laying a live coal on top, they suck at the other end." The smoke, he said, then "streams out of their mouths and nostrils as out of a chimney." Cartier and some of his men tried smoking the herb but did not care for it: "When it is in one's mouth, one would think one had taken powdered pepper, it is so hot."

In the course of time, the Europeans found tobacco being consumed in many different forms throughout the two Americas. Cortes in Mexico saw the emperor Montezuma and Aztec dignitaries smoking elaborate pipes. Others at the emperor's court smoked hollow reeds stuffed with a mixture of tobacco and other dried plant material—cigarettes. The cigarette was popular among Indian people in both Mexico and Central America. Indeed it was an outstanding feature of sophisticated social life among the Aztecs. In the markets of Mexico, Cortes saw men and women selling perfumed cigarettes, decorated pipes, and great quantities of dried tobacco leaves. In the West Indies and parts of South America, Europeans first came across the cigar—a roll of tobacco wrapped in its own leaf. Cigar smoking was common among the Mayas. The Aztecs smoked cigars "inserted in tubes [holders] of tortoise shell or silver." Both in the West Indies and in parts of South America, Indian men snuffed tobacco smoke up both nostrils through a Y-shaped tube. The Aztecs used tobacco in the form of snuff; the Incas used it in no other way. In northwestern North America and parts of South America men crumbled the dried leaves, mixed them with crushed shells and water, and made pellets, which they chewed. In some areas of the Americas tobacco was eaten or mixed with water and taken as a drink.

Many Indian people looked on tobacco as a form of medicine. The Mayas believed it would cure colds, headaches, and snakebites. The Incas used it only as medicine, in the form of snuff. Some tribes west of the Mississippi valued it in treating sores and inflammations of the skin. In several regions it was common to blow smoke into the ear of one who had an earache.

Pipe smoking was the most widespread way that Indian people used tobacco when the first Euopeans arrived. The custom was found in most parts of North America and also

This Mandan pipe, or calumet, has a stone bowl; the wooden stem is 40 inches long. The pipe is decorated with eagle feathers, beadwork, and tufts of horsehair, and dates from the early 1800s. Such a pipe would be used only on cermonial occasions.

along the southeast coast of South America. North American pipes usually consisted of a stone or clay bowl into which a long hollow reed or bone was fastened for a stem. For ceremonial use the stem was decorated with feathers, strands of human hair, beaded bands, and other ornaments. The traders called these pipes calumets, a French word meaning reed or tube. The calumet is often associated with the Dakota or Sioux of the central plains of North America. They regarded the tobacco plant as a gift from the Great Spirit and the bowl as an altar on which the sacred plant was burned. Tobacco was part of almost all their important religious and social ceremonies. In religious rituals they not only smoked tobacco but also cast it on the water to appease evil forces, sprinkled it on the fire as an appeal to the Great Spirit, or buried it with the dead. They smoked the calumet to bind agreements, pledge friendship, and celebrate solemn occasions. As one Indian leader expressed it, "Before talking of holy things, we prepare ourselves by offerings. . . . One will fill his pipe and hand it to another, who will light it and offer it to the sky and earth. . . . They will smoke together; then they will be ready to talk."

The power and importance of the calumet is shown in an

experience which the missionary Louis Hennepin had on an expedition down the Mississippi in the 1600s. Friendly Indians gave Hennepin and his party a calumet, "a most sacred thing amongst them," wrote Hennepin. "It is a large pipe. The head is finely polished, and the quill [stem] which is commonly two foot and a half long, is made of a pretty strong reed or cane, adorned with feathers of all colors, interlaced with locks of women's hair." Such a pipe is "a pass and safe conduct amongst all the allies of the nation who has given it; and in all embassies, ambassadors carry the calumet as the symbol of peace, which is always respected. . . . All their declarations of war or conclusions of peace as well as all other ceremonies are sealed . . . with this calumet. . . . I had certainly perished in my voyage had it not been for this calumet or pipe."

The Indians also smoked for pleasure, the use of tobacco that is best understood today. The first Americans smoked when visitors came, while resting, and in other social situations. Smoking was part of the ceremony at a marriage feast or a conference of elders. One historian remarked, "The Indians never attend a council without a pipe. . . . The smoke, they say, gives them intelligence and enables them to see clearly through the most intricate affairs." An early traveler in western North America told how he was invited to the lodge of an Indian: "The feast was finished and the pipe began to circulate. It was a remarkably large and fine one." On another occasion he wrote, "I found a circle of smokers seated in their usual place; that is, on the ground before the lodge of a certain warrior. . . . There I sat down to smoke a parting pipe with my . . . friends."

We know that the American Indians began using tobacco long, long ago. A Maya temple sculpture of an aged priest smoking a ceremonial pipe has a date corresponding to more than a thousand years before Columbus. Carved pipes of the Mound Builders were found in Ohio, made of material that archaeologists believe came from about the same time.

If smoking was well established then, it must have been started long before. Other evidence of long use is found in the plant itself. Although the tobacco plant has more than fifty varieties, the one the Indian people used most was the mild, big-leafed kind that is almost the only one raised today. Indian people domesticated that kind so long ago that no wild ancestor of the plant has ever been found.

As they domesticated the tobacco plant, the first Americans worked out the many steps in raising it. They also invented the method of curing and aging the leaves so that they taste best for each kind of use. And they invented tobacco pipes, cigars, cigarettes, chewing tobacco, and snuff. The rest of the world took over all this: the domesticated tobacco, the method of raising the plants and processing the leaves, the ways of using the tobacco, and the tools for doing so—even cigarette filters and cigar holders—as invented by the Native Americans and made tobacco the most widely used non-food plant on earth today.

The Spanish invaders in Mexico and South America looked down on most Indian uses of tobacco. The priests condemned the use of tobacco in religious ceremonies; government officials scorned the custom of smoking for pleasure as a vile practice. But the use of tobacco as medicine was something else. Spanish officials not only accepted that but went far beyond the Indian uses and considered tobacco a cure for all diseases. We must remember that in the 1500s and even later American Indian medicine was in many respects more advanced than that in Europe.

In the early 1500s the Spanish took tobacco seeds to Europe, where they started to grow the plant. The leaves were first sold in Spanish and Portuguese apothecary shops as medicine. In 1561 Jean Nicot (nee KO), the French ambassador to Portugal, sent some tobacco back to France. As a result the plant was named for him. The botanical name for tobacco is *Nicotiana* (ni ko shi A na), and the active substance in the leaves is called nicotine.

Although tobacco was used in rituals and ceremonies among many Indian peoples, smoking for pleasure was also a custom with them. We see a fine example of it in this painting of Dakota pipe smokers. *Indian Women in a Tent,* done by Peter Rindisbacher in the early 1800s.

Courtesy West Point Museum Collections, U. S. Military Academy

While the upper classes in Europe still scorned the "heathen" custom of smoking for enjoyment, the habit was being spread to all parts of the globe by sailors. Eventually some members of the upper classes in Europe tried a pipeful or two, to see what it was like. Some must have enjoyed it, for once they started, they kept on. Sir Walter Raleigh is famous for having brought pipe smoking to the court of Queen Elizabeth I. Clerics in Europe at first condemned the custom but after testing the weed took to it with enthusiasm. Scholars and royalty followed suit. Gradually the medical uses of tobacco were forgotten. The social use remained and grew. How it grew!

The Spanish had started raising tobacco in their American possessions by the mid-1500s in order to have supplies for their slaves and sailors. By the end of the century this Indian product was the main crop in the West Indies, and the European market was growing. As smoking for pleasure increased in Europe, some tobacco was raised in almost every country there.

In 1613 the colonist John Rolfe began raising tobacco in Jamestown, Virginia, from plants he had brought from the West Indies. The crop proved such a success that only seven years later Virginia was sending more tobacco to the mother country than England was buying from Spain. Until they started to raise tobacco, the people of Virginia had been desperately poor. Tobacco made them prosper, because it proved to be a cash crop which they could send to England in exchange for goods they needed. In time it became the basis of their whole economy and long took the place of money. It was used to pay taxes, buy goods in the stores, even pay the ministers' salaries. Later, tobacco was also raised in other southern colonies.

As the 1700s progressed and tobacco use increased in Europe, raising and marketing the crop became a permanent part of life in the colonies. The tobacco industry created great plantations, wealth, a sound economy, and leaders who, before the end of the century, would guide the colonies to independence. Thus tobacco played a great part in this early period of United States history.

Tobacco has always been used in all its forms to some extent, but there have been styles of use in certain eras. Today the cigarette is the most popular form, but it has not always been so. The eighteenth century was the age of snuff taking. In the courts and among the wealthy classes in Europe at that time, snuff was almost a way of life. Gold and silver jeweled snuff boxes of that time are greatly prized by museums today. After the American Revolution, citizens of the infant United States threw off such European customs as powdered wigs, cocked hats—and snuff. The hardy pioneers of the time took up chewing tobacco as a widespread custom. Cuspidors or spittoons stood in every hotel lobby, railroad depot, restaurant, office, and in many parlors. Before midcentury, cigar smoking came into fashion. In European wars French and British soldiers picked up the habit from the Spanish. United States soldiers brought back a taste for cigars from the Mexican War in the 1840s. At about the same time, the modern cigarette began its career, not in America, but in Europe. French and British soldiers learned about the smoke from Turkish troops during the Crimean War in the 1850s and brought it home to Paris and London. Soon afterward, cigarette smoking began to grow in popularity, first in Europe, then in America. Sales increased when machines were invented for their manufacture in the 1880s and cigarettes could be sold at a low price—five cents for a box of ten. The use of both cigars and chewing tobacco declined in the early 1900s, as more and more people switched to cigarettes. This took place roughly at the same time as the change from the horse and buggy to the automobile. By the late twentieth century cigarette smoking was part of the lifestyle in most of the world. In the United States, 620 billion cigarettes were consumed in 1976.

Tobacco eventually had a giant effect on almost every

phase of life in many countries. It has affected agriculture, industry, taxation, government regulations, international trade, advertising, commerce, morals, medicine, social customs, and personal habits.

Although tobacco use has grown steadily for the last five hundred years, the custom has called forth protest from many sources. It has been attacked, and defended, by royalty, clergymen, scholars, poets, philosophers, businessmen, doctors, and scientists. Protest began when the Spaniards condemned smoking as a "heathen" practice. Smoking was forbidden in most European countries in the 1500s. During the early 1600s people were even put to death for it in India, Turkey, Russia, China, and Japan. In 1604 King James I of England issued a "counterblaste" against tobacco, but later gave in when he saw how much tax could be collected from the product. Laws against tobacco use were passed in several American colonies, but they were always repealed. Through the 1700s and 1800s antitobacco societies and journals flourished in several lands. In our own country, laws were passed in fourteen states to prohibit tobacco use, but all were later repealed.

Opposition to tobacco use is perhaps stronger today than it has ever been. The protest, however, is not the result of superstition or prejudice, as in earlier times. It is based on scientific findings. As early as the 1930s medical authorities both here and in Europe began to suspect that smoking, especially cigarette smoking, seriously affects health and length of life. In the years since then, the sharp increase in lung cancer and other diseases related to smoking confirmed their suspicions. In 1964 the United States Surgeon General's Advisory Committee declared officially that cigarette smoking is dangerous to health.

Scientific investigation that has been carried on since the 1930s, shows that smoking either causes or contributes to several serious illnesses. Coronary heart disease is the single greatest cause of death among cigarette smokers. It is the most important health hazard caused by smoking. Chronic bronchitis is another disease that is closely linked to smoking. In the United States, smoking has been found to be the principal cause of this disease. Clinical studies show that cancer is also closely connected with smoking. Cigarette smokers are ten times more likely to develop lung cancer than are nonsmokers. A large percentage of cases are related to tobacco use. Research also reveals a strong link between various forms of tobacco use and cancer of the mouth and throat. In addition, cigarette smokers are more likely to contract other diseases than are those who do not smoke. They are sick more days of the year, and they die at an earlier age than do nonsmokers.

Tobacco smoke is harmful to the body because it is composed of various gases, many of which are poisonous, and because of tiny particles of matter it contains. The most deadly gas in smoke is carbon monoxide. If this gas is breathed in a pure form, it kills a person in a very short time. The harmful particles of matter in tobacco smoke are mainly tar and nicotine. Tar is made up of hundreds of chemicals, which include most of the known cancer-causing agents in cigarette smoke. Nicotine, a strong poison, is the habit-forming element in tobacco. When cigarette smoke is inhaled, 70 percent of the tar and nicotine particles remain in the lungs. Although carbon monoxide and nicotine are both harmful, strong evidence suggests that the combination contributes to the development of heart disease.

Inhaling smoke clearly increases the ill effects of smoking. When a filter cigarette is used, the amount of harmful material that enters the mouth and lungs is reduced. Even so, studies show that a filter cigarette smoker is four times as likely to get lung cancer as a nonsmoker.

Cigar and pipe smokers usually do not inhale the smoke, and for that reason they suffer less danger to their lungs. But they still risk getting cancer of the mouth and throat and are more subject to heart disease.

Death rates are not as high among those who smoke cigarettes that have less tar and nicotine, yet they are higher than the rates among nonsmokers. In an attempt to protect the public, the American Cancer Society has, since 1970, supported research into the development of a less dangerous cigarette. The tobacco industry is making use of the techniques for manufacturing such a cigarette.

Today more people than ever before are aware of the injurious effects of smoking and, for that reason, are giving up the habit or are smoking less. Unfortunately, however, the harmful consequences of tobacco use are often slow to appear. And thus it is hard for many people to see that ill health or premature death may result from smoking. The bad effects of tobacco use are sometimes not felt for many years. By that time, the smoker is sorry that he or she was so foolish as to have smoked, but the damage has been done.

Because of the link between smoking and disease, the Federal Trade Commission ruled in 1964 that all cigarette packages must bear a warning that tobacco use may injure the smoker's health. A further step was taken in 1970 when cigarette advertising was banned from television, especially because of the influence it might have on children and young people. Many federal, state, and other agencies have adopted regulations that limit smoking in public places. More than thirty countries are trying to curb excessive smoking by their citizens. Great Britain has restricted tobacco advertising. Finland has prohibited it altogether. Sweden is trying to eliminate cigarette smoking by the year 2000. Russia, Poland, and West Germany are taking similar steps to protect their people against the hazards of tobacco use.

In recent years, for the first time, non-Indian people have found a use for tobacco that the Indian people did not invent. Scientists have discovered that the plant can be an important source of protein that is sorely needed for human food. With the explosive increase in the world's population, governments are looking desperately for new, easily produced sources of protein to feed the hungry. Experiments with corn and other plants give promising results. Tobacco, it is believed, will be especially valuable for this purpose; it is the only plant from which protein can be extracted in pure form.

Green leafy plants are nature's most abundant source of protein. But each separate leaf contains very little of the substance. To be made into a useful form, the protein must be extracted from the leaves and then concentrated. Proteins made from tobacco are rich sources of nourishment. One kind may prove of great value in diets for patients suffering from certain diseases of the kidney, liver, and heart.

When tobacco is raised for food, several important advantages appear. A farmer who raises smoking tobacco sets out 8,000 plants per acre. If he raised tobacco for food, he could plant as many as 150,000 plants on an acre, or nearly twenty times as many. Besides this, he could harvest two crops every season. The young leaves are cut six weeks after planting; four weeks later, another crop can be taken. This would produce a much higher income than the present tobacco farmer enjoys.

Processing tobacco leaves for protein also results in a number of valuable by-products. Some of the material that is left after protein has been extracted from the leaves can be added to animal feed. The nicotine that is removed can be used in the manufacture of insecticides. Other remains can be made into smoking products of proved quality and safety, products that do not have most of the elements considered dangerous to health.

Tobacco has another great advantage over other plants as a source of food. It already grows in many countries. Varieties have been developed that can be grown successfully around the world, from the equator to northern Siberia.

Until now, the extraction and concentration of protein from tobacco leaves have taken place only in scientific laboratories. To do this commercially, on a large scale, will call for the building of factories and machinery and the creation of a new industry. Before the end of the century, tobacco grown for food may become a major agricultural product. This Indian crop will then continue to play a part in world economy, trade, government, and industry, but it will also help to feed the hungry and contribute to human health and welfare. Another Indian gift.

11
Cotton and Other Fibers and American Dyes

COTTON, THE world's most important vegetable fiber, was domesticated on both sides of the world. It was raised in India thousands of years ago; later its cultivation spread to other countries in Asia and beyond. By the Middle Ages cotton cloth was being sold in Europe, but it was an expensive luxury because it had to be imported from Asia.

Meanwhile cotton was also being raised, spun, and woven in the Americas. Columbus found cotton growing in the West Indies when he first landed. Indians there offered him cotton yarn for barter, and he saw "great quantities of cotton gathered, spun, and worked up." He knew that the plant was raised in the Indies, and this helped to convince him he had reached that region of the world. He took samples of cotton to the king and queen of Spain as "proof" that he had reached the Indies. The admiral mentions seeing people with "their heads wrapped in scarves of cotton, worked elaborately in colors." He also speaks of "handkerchiefs of cotton, very symmetrically [evenly] woven, and worked in colors."

In Mexico not many years later Cortes found that the Aztecs had an extensive cotton textile industry. Among the gifts the emperor Montezuma gave him were "many rich garments of cotton and featherwork, marvelously woven, unequaled in color and design, beyond anything the Spaniards had ever seen." At another time Montezuma gave the conquistador "curtains, coverlets, and robes of cotton, fine as silk, of rich and various dyes. . . . More than 30 loads of cotton cloth in addition." Cortes's men saw cotton mantles, bed covers, draperies, skirts, pants, tablecloths, and handkerchiefs for sale in the marketplaces of Mexico. One early Spanish historian wrote that the Aztec women were "well clothed, beautifully adorned. All had wonderfully wrought skirts and pretty *huipilli* [blouses]." The Aztec men dressed in long woven cloaks knotted at the shoulder. Priests wore long black ponchos.

The people of Mexico spun and wove several grades of cotton, not only for clothes but also for hammocks, ropes, grain sacks, and other articles. A heavy cotton cloth, made into thickly quilted jackets, was so tough that it could stop the sharp point of a flying arrow and serve as armor. Cortes had such jackets made for his troops, who learned to prefer them to the heavy metal armor they had brought from Europe.

None of this material survives today. We know of it from written records, murals from the time of the Aztecs, and paintings on pottery, sculpture, and drawings dating from the era.

Well-preserved plant remains, dug up in the Mexican desert in more recent times, show that cotton was being raised there more than five thousand years ago. Some of the plants that were found are upland cotton, the kind that still grows there.

From Mexico the cultivation of cotton spread northward to our present Southwest—Arizona, New Mexico, and the surrounding area. This took place possibly more than two thousand years ago. When the Spanish arrived in the 1500s, the Pueblo Indians there had been growing cotton on irrigated land for many centuries. Because of the very dry climate, a large amount of cotton cloth from early ages was preserved in caves, cliff dwellings, pueblos, and graves. A few pieces were made as early as A.D. 700, but most are dated between 1000 and 1400. Thus all were made before the arrival of the Spanish. Nearly a thousand pieces were found in more than a hundred sites. Some were mere shreds, but others were large, perfect pieces. They included many garments and various kinds of weaves, both plain and intricate. The biggest fabrics were those found in graves, for the dead were often wrapped in large pieces of cloth. These and the clothes buried with the dead help to give people of today a clear idea of the accomplishments of the ancient cotton spinners and weavers.

The cultivation and use of cotton may have reached far beyond the Southwest. At least one example suggests that it did: Champlain recorded that Iroquois soldiers, several thousand miles away on the north Atlantic coast, wore quilted cotton armor like that of the Aztecs.

In South America the first European invaders found Indian people raising cotton in several regions. Portuguese soldiers saw fields of cotton in Brazil; others saw the plant growing in Paraguay. When the Spanish came to Peru, the Inca government had a large weaving industry, producing goods both from cotton and from the fleece of the llama and related animals. The invaders were struck by the fineness of the Inca cotton goods. Large government warehouses were filled with the material, much of it dyed in brilliant colors. We do not have to rely wholly on records for information about the Inca fabrics, for many beautiful pieces have survived to the present.

In more recent times cotton mantles, robes, veils, and other garments, discovered in ancient graves along the coast of Peru, show that cotton was raised there more than four thousand years ago. The cotton that was grown in Central and South America and the West Indies is the kind now called sea island. It is the finest cotton in the world. Its glossy fiber, or staple, up to two inches long, can be spun into a thread as fine as a spider's web, and the cloth woven from it is smooth and soft as silk. In fact, the Spanish thought the cotton cloth of the Incas was silk.

The Europeans adopted the cottons of the Americas, just as they took over so many other things of value from the Indian people. The commercial cottons of the world today were developed from the two kinds domesticated by the first Americans—upland and sea island. Gradually these two varieties replaced Old World cottons and became the basis of a great industry that has affected the history of many nations.

Before the end of the 1500s the Portuguese were raising cotton in Brazil to send to Europe. The Spanish were raising it for the same purpose in the West Indies. In the 1600s English colonists along the Atlantic began planting small patches of cotton for home use; they probably raised the upland variety now common throughout the South. Homespun was then the only kind of cloth. Colonial women had spun and woven flax and wool in their homes in Europe and had brought their spinning wheels and looms to America. Most families in the colonies raised small fields of flax and kept a few sheep to provide fiber for clothes, household linens, rope, grain sacks, and other needs. In the warmer southern colonies it was easy to add cotton plants to the gardens so that the women could also spin and weave cotton.

By the 1600s some cotton cloth was being made in England out of raw material from Asia, Brazil, and the West Indies. The work of spinning and weaving was a cottage industry there, carried on in homes. During the 1700s, however, machines were invented that made it possible to manufacture cloth much faster than before. This brought about a great need for more raw material. The American colonists did not increase their crop, however, because they were faced with the problem of how to take the seeds out of the cotton. Their problem was solved in 1793 when Eli Whitney invented the cotton gin. A gin that was powered by a steam engine could remove the seeds from a thousand pounds of cotton a day. At once the farmers in the South began to plant more cotton; there was a market for all they could produce. Most of their crop was sent to the textile mills in England, where American cotton was greatly preferred to the rough, short-staple kinds that grew in the Old World.

In the late 1700s textile mills were built in the United States, adding to the demand for this American Indian crop. Most of the mills were built in New England where they soon formed the region's largest industry, second only to England's. As a result, raising cotton became very profitable. Here is another Indian crop that had a great effect on the course of events in the United States. It is part of the history of our country.

Since work in the fields depended on cheap labor, the growers brought in more and more slaves from Africa. Before many years, cotton was king in the South, and 60 percent of the slaves worked in the cotton fields. This American Indian product was so profitable that in the South it produced a one-crop economy, which became one cause of the Civil War.

The United States was the world's greatest cotton producer from the early 1800s until the 1960s. Since then, Russia's production has in most years been larger. The cotton domesticated by the American Indians is also raised in more than seventy other countries. American upland cotton accounts for seven-eighths of the world's commercial crop. Sea island accounts for most of the rest. This gift from the American Indians adds billions of dollars to the world's wealth each year, besides adding beautiful and useful articles to our lives.

Most cotton raised in the United States and nearly all that is raised in the rest of the world is American upland, which has a strong, medium-length staple and a high yield per acre. Sea island, which has a long, silky staple, is grown in some southwestern states, the West Indies, Peru, and Egypt.

Egypt is today the world's main supplier of long-staple cotton. A variety of sea island taken there in 1821 is among

The Egyptian cotton being tended here is a variety of the plant that was domesticated centuries ago by the American Indians.

American Cotton Grower

the world's finest. This American Indian crop, planted on one-third of the nation's cultivated land, forms the basis of Egypt's economy.

Several other valuable products come from the cotton plant besides fibers. Linters, the fuzz left on the seeds after ginning, are used in making guncotton, photographic film, mattresses, and cotton batting. Seed hulls go into the making of stock feed, fertilizers, fuel, and packing material. Fiber from the stalks is made into cardboard. Cottonseed, once looked on as a nuisance, is such a valuable by-product that processing it is a large, separate industry. The seeds are pressed to obtain oil, which is used in the manufacture of some kinds of food; it is also used in paint, soap, cosmetics, and detergents. The seed cake, left after the oil has been pressed out, is a rich feed for cattle.

In the 1960s a new and important use for cottonseed was discovered, when scientists found a way to make a high-quality protein flour from the seeds. In the future this product may become an important source of the protein that is so badly needed to feed humanity.

Cotton is not the only fiber that the world obtained in the Americas. The Inca people had several kinds of woolen cloth that the Spaniards had never seen before. It was spun and woven from the fleece of the llama, alpaca, and vicuña (ve KOON ya), small beasts native to the Andes. The wool of the guanaco (gwah NAH ko) was sometimes also used. Although the Spanish called them Peruvian sheep, the animals are not sheep but small humpless camels.

The Inca and pre-Inca people used the fleece of the llama, which is coarser than that of the alpaca and vicuña, to make blankets, ropes, strong sacks for holding produce, and clothes for the common people. The Spanish learned to use the wool, and the llama is still raised for its wool in Peru.

The alpaca, smaller than the llama, is not much larger than a sheep. Its fleece is fine and soft, and so long that it sometimes reaches the ground. The Incas made it into elegant fabrics for royalty and hangings for their temples and palaces. Today Peru leads the world in the production of alpaca fleece, which is still used for luxury fabrics.

The vicuña, the smallest of the animals, has the silkiest fleece of all. From it the Inca weavers made the most precious cloth for robes and hangings to be used in temples and the royal household. One early historian wrote that the richly colored cloth "of the delicate manufacture of the Peruvian wool . . . was of so beautiful a texture that the Spanish sovereigns, with all the luxury of Europe and Asia at their command, did not disdain to use it." Cloth woven from vicuña fleece is still considered the most luxurious in the world. Today the fleece is exported from Peru, Bolivia, and Chile.

Of less importance, yet worthy to be mentioned, are other kinds of fiber that the Indian people of Mexico taught the Europeans to use. They are fibers taken from various tropical plants, which both Mayas and Aztecs made into coarse cloth, sandals, ropes, fish line, bowstrings, and other articles. One of them is sisal (SIGH sal). When the machine grain binder was invented in the 1880s, this Indian product proved to be an ideal material for binder twine to tie bundles of grain as it was cut in the field. Sisal fiber is also made into ropes and cords, woven into porch rugs, and used for the bristles of coarse brushes. Most sisal is now raised in Brazil and Africa. Fibers of the maguey (MAG way) plant, with roughly the same uses, were also used by both Mayas and Aztecs and taken over by the Europeans. The plant is still raised in Mexico today.

The American Indians, who were so skilled in spinning and weaving, were also expert in creating dyes from plant and animal substances. A modern scientist has listed 250 plants in Peru alone from which dyes were made. Nearly 200 different shades and tints have been counted in ancient Peruvian textiles.

The Spaniards learned about Indian dyes soon after they invaded Mexico and South America. They realized at once the value of the products and sent many galleons loaded with rich cargoes of the products back to Spain. Good dyes were in great demand for coloring not only cloth but also cosmetics, paper, inks, artists' supplies, glass, leather, and furniture wood. Natural dyes were the only kind known until the mid-1800s, when scientists began to create dyes out of chemicals.

Colors are also made from dyewoods, of which several kinds are native to the Americas. One of the best is brazilwood, from which the Mayas made red, purple, and brown dyes. It had been exported to Europe for centuries from the Near East. When Portuguese explorers found a similar wood in South America, they gave the name Brazil to the place where it grew. Brazilwood is still used to make red ink and to stain other woods for certain furniture. Logwood, grown in Central America, was valued for the black dye that can be made from it.

The seed pulp of a Mexican tree provided the Aztecs with a bright yellow dye that the Spanish found to be excellent for coloring cloth. Known as annatto (an NOT toe), or arnotto, it has been used in more recent times to color butter, cheese, oleomargarine, and other foods.

The most highly prized dye created by the Native Americans is cochineal (koch i NEEL), a rich crimson made from dried insects. The Mayas raised the insects in plantations of cactus on which the insects fed. The Spanish were impressed with the unusual beauty and value of the dye and exported it to many countries. In Europe, where it soon took the place of most other red dyes, it was especially prized by the English textile industry. Today cochineal has been replaced by synthetic dyes for most uses, but it is still considered the best coloring for red ink, lipstick, and certain drinks. Until as late as 1954 cochineal was used to produce the traditional scarlet color of British guards' uniforms.

Part III

CHAPTER
12

American Indian Inventions

THE AMERICAN Indians invented many clever and valuable objects and processes. The rest of the world could not use some of them, such as the Inca system for keeping records by means of knotted strings, called quipus (KEE pooz). Some objects and procedures, such as spinning, weaving, and the wheel, were invented in both hemispheres. But the rest of the world has found other American Indian inventions very useful.

Before we describe them, let us ask: What is an invention? An invention may be an object, like a compass, or a substance, such as paper. It may be a process, like printing; it may be an idea, like the idea of zero, represented by 0. An invention may also be a discovery, and it is not always possible to tell one from the other.

Many Indian inventions were described in earlier chapters of this book, in connection with other subjects. Rubber is one example. Indians in the American tropics invented the process of making rubber and ways of using it. These have been wholeheartedly accepted by the world.

Mankind adopted the tobacco plant from the Indian people and ways of treating and using it. This includes many inventions. Present-day cigars are made by rolling tobacco in a leaf from the plant, like the cigars first seen by Columbus's men. Some Indian people made cigarettes by stuffing tobacco into a hollow reed or by rolling it in cornhusks—the same principle that is used in making today's cigarettes. Smokers today copy Indians by using filters, cigar holders, and snuff.

One explorer writing in the 1600s described how the Indians built duck blinds for hunting and made decoys by stuffing the feathered skins of fowl or carving wooden figures of birds. These Indian inventions, soon adopted by the early colonists, are still used. Today's hikers hold their backpacks in place with a tumpline across the forehead—another Indian invention. The design of the Dakota tepee was adapted by General Henry H. Sibley to become the Sibley tent, long part of U. S. Army equipment.

Cochineal, annatto, and other dyes—or the processes for making them—may be considered inventions, as may the many plant compounds and extracts that were found useful as medicines.

This duck decoy, still in remarkably good condition, was made by an Indian hunter of the desert culture two or three thousand years ago. It was found in west central Nevada.
Courtesy, Museum of the American Indian, Heye Foundation

Many Indian inventions have to do with food. Two examples are the process of making chocolate out of cacao seeds and the fermenting of vanilla pods to produce the vanilla flavor. Another is the invention of what we call Cracker Jack. A Jesuit missionary in the 1600s reported that the Huron Indians of eastern Canada made this snack by pouring maple syrup over popcorn. Of more importance perhaps is the process of taking the poison out of bitter cassava. Indians of the tropics invented that procedure, as well as the grater and press for carrying it out.

Corn and the many ways of preparing it may be considered inventions. In harvesting maize, the first Americans invented the husking pin, part of every farmer's harvesting equipment until the early 1900s. The building we know as the corncrib was designed by the Indian people as a place to store their corn while it dried. The Europeans adopted the design of the building, with its ventilated sides, and it can still be seen on farms in the Corn Belt.

The Maya nation, which achieved the highest civilization of any people in the Americas, made two remarkable inventions. These should be mentioned even though they were also made in the Eastern Hemisphere. They are the idea of zero and the calendar.

The zero was invented in three different civilizations, those of the Babylonians, the Mayas, and the Hindus. These three peoples each invented a way of writing large numbers as a series of small numbers, or digits. For instance, if we write 749, the 7 means 700, the 4 means 40 and the 9 means 9. If we write 709, we need the zero to hold the empty place in the series. We use the number system invented by the Hindus, which was improved by the Arabs, then passed on to Europe. Neither the ancient Greeks nor the Romans had such a system. Until Europeans started using Arabic numbers, they struggled along with the crude, clumsy Roman numerals. To show you how unsatisfactory they are, try multiplying XXIV by VIII, instead of using the Arabic 24×8.

The Mayas had a number system using zero a thousand years before the Arabs perfected the one we now use.

The other great invention, the calendar, was also made possible by the mathematical genius of the Mayas. More than two thousand years ago their astronomers created a calendar that was very nearly as accurate as the one we have today and far more accurate than the one used by the Spanish when they invaded Mexico. These two inventions, zero and the calendar, place the Maya people among the most advanced thinkers in early history.

We know that the first Americans invented the wheel, because many small wheeled objects formed of clay have been found in excavations in Mexico. No one can say with certainty what they were used for, but it is generally believed that they were tops. In any case, the people of ancient Mexico probably did not use wheels on vehicles for transportation like those in the Eastern Hemisphere, because they had no horses or other draft animals.

The Indian people did, however, invent means of transportation, some of which were adopted by the rest of the world. Among these is the birchbark canoe. This craft, in some ways the finest invention that the Europeans took from the Americans, was created by those who lived in the forest and lake country and who needed a craft to travel on water. Since various kinds of birch trees grew plentifully in their region, some clever, imaginative persons must have noticed that the bark of the tree is flexible, tough, lightweight, and water-

These two clay figures, each about 10 inches long, show that the American Indians did invent the wheel. These and many similar objects, found in excavations throughout Mexico, may be toys. Those pictured here date from the year 800 to 1250.

Courtesy Museum of the American Indian, Heye Foundation

proof. Also, the birch wears its bark "like a loose golden vest," which is easily removed. This may have led to the invention and perfecting of the craft we know as the birchbark canoe. The boat is a light wooden frame of unusually clever design, with a covering of bark. Various kinds of birch were used, the white birch being preferred. The Ojibwa, around the western Great Lakes, were especially skilled at building and handling the craft. They needed it for hunting, fishing, harvesting wild rice, traveling for trade, seasonal moving, and other purposes. It was as indispensable to them as the automobile is to us today.

The first white explorers who sailed along the north Atlantic coast of North America were amazed to see the slender, graceful canoes of the Indians glide out toward their ships. Their own heavy longboats, lowered from the decks and manned by four or more sailors who labored at the oars, were no match for the Indian craft, which skimmed over the water leaving hardly a ripple. The Europeans were especially impressed by the lightness and speed of the canoe and its ability to carry heavy loads in shallow water. They were astonished at the skill of paddlers who took the craft safely down swirling rapids.

Cartier was the first European to describe the canoe. He saw the craft when he explored the St. Lawrence in the early 1500s. Champlain, a century later, saw hundreds of bark canoes and mentioned them often in his travel accounts. He wrote more than once that the canoes could go faster than his own well-manned boats. Champlain at once recognized the superior qualities of the canoe and saw that it was the only vehicle that could successfully travel the forest waters of the north: "He who would pass the rapids must provide himself with the canoes of the Indians which a man can easily carry . . . with the canoes . . . one may travel freely and quickly throughout the country, as well up the little rivers as up the big ones." Champlain is responsible for persuading the French to adopt the Indian canoe for exploring

The birchbark canoe is the remarkable invention of the North American Indians of the northeastern lake country. They used it for hunting, fishing, traveling for trade or pleasure, and many other purposes. The group shown in this painting *Chippewa Family in Canoe* by Eastman Johnson might be on their way to visit relatives. The painting was made in the mid-1800s.

and fur trading. French traders, explorers, missionaries, artists, scientists, and soldiers all depended on the canoe for their travels in North America.

There is no doubt that the birchbark canoe made possible the rapid growth and success of the highly profitable fur trade that flourished between the white men and the Indians in North America from the early 1600s until nearly 1900. Each spring brigades of canoes left cities along the St. Lawrence, loaded with guns, traps, kettles, beads, and other supplies bound for trading posts in western Indian country. There they exchanged their cargo for packs of the furs that

had accumulated in the winter past, bringing them back to the river ports from where they were sent to Europe.

French traders hired Indian craftsmen to make canoes for them and teach them how to build and handle the boats. To make sure they would have a dependable supply, one trading company opened a "factory" at the settlement of Three Rivers on the St. Lawrence in the early 1700s. There the various kinds of canoes were built to order, out of materials from the forest. The biggest were the huge Montreal boats, 36 to 40 feet long, each of which held a cargo of five tons. In spite of their great size, these remarkable craft weighed less than 300 pounds and could be carried over the roughest portages between waterways or around waterfalls by three or four men. Smaller canoes were built to transport goods and men on lesser lakes and streams.

In 1763, when they were defeated by the English, the French had to leave Canada. The English then took over the vast fur trade that had been started by the French and continued using Indian canoes to transport furs from the inland trading posts to the Atlantic. The canoe remained part of the fur trade until the late 1800s, when the means of transportation were finally modernized.

Although the historic role of the canoe in nearly three centuries of the fur trade has ended, the canoe of the first Americans is as useful as ever. The art of building birchbark canoes is practiced today by only a few craftsmen, for most of today's canoes are machine-made. Thousands are manufactured each year in Europe and America, for sport or recreation. Even though they are built of modern materials, the design of the present-day craft is the same as that of the boats created by the Indian people long ago. All who enjoy canoeing, and there are many thousands throughout the world, are grateful for the gift of this splendid American Indian invention.

For land travel in the northern regions, the Indian supplied the white men with other inventions. One was the snowshoe. Champlain says of this device that "when the snows are heavy, they make a kind of raquet . . . which they fasten to their feet and so walk on snow without sinking, for otherwise they could not hunt, nor make their way in many places." Indian people would not have been able to survive in the snowy northern regions without this ancient invention. Wearing snowshoes, they could travel long distances over deep snow in forest or open country.

The origin of the snowshoe is lost in the mists of time, for the invention was well developed when the Europeans made the first records of it in America. It was the Indians of Canada who perfected the device. They designed dozens of styles, some say hundreds, to suit every kind of travel need and every kind of snow. Artists of early times made many paintings of Indian people hunting and traveling while wearing snowshoes.

The snowshoe is made by bending a strip or branch of tough wood—such as ash, maple, or hickory—and bringing

The canoes used today for sport or recreation are manufactured from modern materials, but the design of the craft is the same as that of the canoes created by Indian people long ago.

Courtesy Minnesota Department of Natural Resources

the ends together to make an oval frame that looks something like a large tennis racquet. The space inside the frame is webbed or woven with strong twine or strips of rawhide to form the footrest. Snowshoes are held on by thongs through which the wearers slip their feet.

White trappers, traders, settlers, missionaries, and later surveyors and lumberjacks learned that they also could not travel in winter without snowshoes. Taking yet another lesson from the first Americans, the white men learned to wear snowshoes while waging war. During the French and Indian Wars, the French were at one point so successful in raiding British settlements—on snowshoes—that the British decided to copy them. In 1758 the English scout Robert Rogers and his men proved the worth of the invention in the so-called Battle of Snowshoes near Lake George. After that, military leaders realized how important snowshoes could be, and the northern colonies made them part of the regular equipment of their military forces.

Even today nothing has replaced the snowshoe. It is widely used for sport and travel, especially in Alaska and Canada.

Since the Indian people designed snowshoes to be worn with moccasins, the Europeans adopted the moccasin for that purpose, if they had not already done so for comfort on the trail. Indians made moccasins for the white people and taught them how to make the Indian shoes. Even today many people enjoy the comfort of manufactured shoes patterned after the moccasin.

To transport goods over ice and snow, the white men adopted the Indian's toboggan. Many of the early Europeans in America mention this clever invention. As Champlain describes it: "They are in the habit of making a kind of wooden sled on which they place their loads and draw them behind without any difficulty, and they go along very quickly." Europeans in the northern regions found the toboggan of the Indians useful for the same purpose.

Indians of North America invented the snowshoe, which they needed for travel on snow. Seth Eastman's painting *Hunting Buffalo in Winter* demonstrates one use of the device by the Dakota people, for whom the buffalo was a major resource.

Courtesy James J. Hill Reference Library, St. Paul.

In building their forts and trading posts, the white men copied the Indians' palisades—rows of logs placed upright in the ground for protection. Champlain describes one village surrounded by a triple palisade 35 feet high. Of another he says, "Their village was enclosed with four stout palisades made of large timbers 30 feet in height, interlaced together, with not more than half a foot between, and galleries like a parapet which they had fitted with double timbers." Although this means of protection may also have been used in other parts of the world, it was the Indians' invention that was adopted by the Europeans in the Americas.

American Indian clothes that were adopted by the Europeans, besides the moccasin, are the poncho and the parka. The parka is the hooded jacket worn by northern people in both hemispheres, but copied by the Europeans from the North Americans. The poncho, invented by people of South America and still worn there, is a blanket with a slit for the head. When not worn as a cape, it can be used as a bed blanket or as a wrapping for a child, or it can be put to other uses. Both the poncho and the parka are standard wear for the U.S. armed forces—the parka for winter wear in the North and the rubberized poncho as a raincoat. Both are also widely used by civilians.

An interesting Indian invention adopted by the rest of the world is the hammock. The story of the hammock is in some ways like that of the canoe. Columbus saw hammocks many times on his voyages. He mentioned them in his accounts and used them himself, calling them "nets in which the Indians sleep, called *hamacas.*" The Italian explorer Amerigo Vespucci saw hammocks in South America and wrote in 1504: "They sleep in certain nets made of cotton, very big and hung in the air." He saw the advantages of the invention and expressed his appreciation of it: "Although this way of sleeping may appear uncomfortable, I say it is a soft way to sleep; we frequently slept in them, and we slept better than in quilts."

The hammock is believed to have been invented by the people of Brazil or other tropical area of the Americas. Certainly the swinging net is a perfect invention for sleeping in the damp jungle, where bugs and other crawling creatures can get into a bed placed on the ground. A hammock is the coolest kind of bed as well, for in it the whole body is exposed to the air. It is an ideal cradle for infants and children, who enjoy gently swinging in the net. Most Indian peoples living in the American tropics used the hammock. When traveling they would roll it up and carry it. In Peru, leaders traveled from one city to another, carried in hammocks.

The Europeans saw that the hammock was one more thing they could adopt from the Indian, and they began to use it soon after they arrived. When La Condamine was in Peru, he found hammocks in the homes of rich Spanish colonists; some ladies would spend most of the day lying in them. The Spanish also saw that the hammock would be a convenient bed for sailors on shipboard, and they at once put it to use in their navy. Before that time, sailors slept wherever they could find a spot on the ship. The hammock is lightweight, easy to make, can be rolled up and carried, takes only a small space to use or store, and costs little. In a sailing vessel it would swing with the roll of the ship. Before 1600 the hammock had become standard equipment for sailors on most European ships. Queen Elizabeth I introduced the device into the Royal Navy in 1597. The Dutch, French, and other Europeans followed suit and used hammocks on their ships for centuries. Ships of the American colonies also were equipped with hammocks, probably following the example of the British.

The U.S. Navy used hammocks until the 1940s. When old ships were replaced during World War II by more modern vessels, they were furnished with bunks instead of hammock hooks, and the use of hammocks gradually came to an end. Most other navies of the world have also abandoned hammocks as shipboard beds. The British navy gave them up in the 1950s after three and a half centuries of use. The Spanish still use hammocks in a few of their vessels and in some naval buildings.

Although most sailors no longer swing as they sleep, the hammock is still with us. We use it to enjoy a leisurely rest on a summer afternoon, and it has been popular for that purpose for many years. The hammock was brought to England in the mid-1800s and advertised as "a luxurious novelty in the way of a substitute for garden chairs." It is still used in that way in both Europe and America. People who live and travel in the tropics also enjoy it as a comfortable, convenient bed.

An unusual use for an ancient Indian invention has been found in more recent times. It is the work of Dr. Madge Skelly, an Iroquois woman on the faculty of St. Louis University. As a specialist in communication, Dr. Skelly worked with adults and children who could not speak because of low mentality or for other reasons. Trying to find a way in which her patients could make themselves understood, she recalled the sign language of the Plains Indians.

This way of communicating developed centuries ago, when tribes that spoke different languages came together for trade or other purposes. Doing extensive research and experiments, Dr. Skelly chose and adapted signs from this complicated language and created a practical system of communication for her patients. She called it Amer-Ind hand talk. Its 250 signs, mostly natural gestures, easily learned and understood, can be combined to express almost any common meaning.

When taught to those who were unable to make themselves understood in any other way, it proved wonderfully effective. After Dr. Skelly's initial success in the 1970s, the system was taken up in more and more hospitals and special schools. A decade later, of the million or so individuals in the United States who cannot use spoken language, more than three thousand are expressing themselves in Amer-Ind hand talk. The sign language has rescued them from the isolation imposed by their handicap, has made it possible for them to reach others, and is opening a new life for them.

These Indian inventions have proved of value to the world. Still others may be found useful in the future.

CHAPTER
13
Indian Contributions to Sports and Recreation

As WE have seen, the first Europeans who came to the New World had to learn how to live like the Native Americans in order to stay alive. They had to eat Indian food prepared by Indian methods, travel on Indian trails, use Indian means of travel, wear the moccasins and buckskins of the Indians, and adopt many other Indian ways. The early scouts and frontiersmen followed Indian ways almost entirely, and many left accounts of how they enjoyed it. Daniel Boone and Davy Crockett are well-known examples, but there were many others.

One of the most important skills that the colonists learned from the first Americans was hunting. Some Indian peoples living north of Mexico hunted for much of their food, and those who did so were usually expert hunters. Most English colonists did not know how to hunt when they came to America. In Europe, during the 1600s and 1700s, hunting was a gentleman's recreation, a sport of royalty and the rich. Deer and other wild animals were kept on private estates and royal preserves, and anyone who shot the game without permission was severely punished. "Hunting is for great men —not for every base, inferior person," wrote an English author in the early 1600s. The colonists, who were not "great men," had had no chance in Europe to learn how to hunt. In America they were forced to do so, not for sport but for food, and the Indians taught them how.

As the European settlements spread westward from the Atlantic, Indian people taught the settlers the many hunting techniques they had devised: duck blinds, moose calls, snares, decoys, fish traps; methods for tracking and stalking game; Indian snowshoes, canoes, toboggans, backpacks with tumplines—all were used.

In the course of time, when the Europeans had taken the lands of the Native Americans and had established farms and communities, they no longer needed the Indian skills. Gradually, much of the original Indian way of life disappeared, as it was affected by the non-Indian culture. Yet that life-style left a deep impression that can still be clearly seen.

The average non-Indian in the United States today thinks of the Indian life of earlier times as adventuresome, romantic, even ideal. Present-day athletics, recreations, and sports, for example, all owe their special character to elements of American Indian culture. Learning to live in the wilds "like an Indian" is considered important to the character development of a young person. The Boy Scout and Girl Scout movements and the Campfire Girl organization have drawn heavily on Indian activities and ideals. The founder of the Campfire Girls said, "the great American inheritance of Indian lore enriched" the organization. The youth organization Woodcraft Indians, founded by Ernest Thompson Seton, "with a program of Indian games, skills, and rituals," was taken into the Boy Scout movement. Seton, a well-known writer and outdoorsman, was long active in scouting; one of his many books on Indian life is dedicated to the Boy Scouts. Another figure important in the history of scouting is Charles Eastman, a Dakota Indian who was born in a tepee and did not see a white man until he was sixteen. Although he later graduated from college and obtained a medical degree from Boston University, Dr. Eastman wrote many books describing his early Indian life. He was active in the scout movement, and his books, especially *Indian Scout Talks*, are still read and studied by scouts. Both Boy Scouts and Girl Scouts instituted Indian lore merit badges. The Boy Scout program also includes badges in canoeing, wilderness survival, and camping that teach Indian ways of life. Indian influence is also seen in the badges dealing with corn, cotton, athletics, and sports.

In addition to organized youth groups, many families and individuals who like outdoor life learn and follow Indian ways. Popular books with titles such as *Living like Indians* teach young readers cleanliness, hardiness, self-reliance, and other principles of conduct that Indian cultures emphasized. Trained leaders are hired to teach young people the same skills that Indians taught the first Europeans: how to handle a canoe, make camp, find their way through the forest, read the signs of changing weather, know the habits of wildlife.

Many adults consider a temporary return to the wilds the most enjoyable kind of vacation. Men and women will leave their comfortable homes to spend a week or two living in a tent, sleeping on the ground, and cooking over a campfire. They feel lucky if they have a "real" Indian guide to help paddle their canoe and catch fish or shoot deer. The hunting techniques that the Native American once used to obtain food now serve the sportsman. Back home, the hunters proudly entertain guests with roast canvasback or venison and wild rice—Indian foods.

Other American Indian customs and objects add to our enjoyment on vacations. The canoe provides recreation; the hammock adds enjoyment to our leisure. The barbecue, the clambake, the bean feed—all come from the American Indian. Even the foods we like to eat while enjoying sports and recreation—peanuts, popcorn, chewing gum, chocolate, Cracker Jack—are Indian.

Sports, which are such a big part of the American scene, would be far different without the influence and contribu-

A side wall of one of several hundred stone ball courts found from Arizona southward to the West Indies, on which Indian teams played using a heavy rubber ball. Although the court is in ruins, the carved ring through which the ball had to pass has survived. The court is in the ancient Maya city of Chichén Itzá, built in Yucatán, Mexico, in the fifth century.

tions of the first Americans. The most important and far-reaching influence on present-day sports throughout the world came about because of an Indian invention—the rubber ball. Indian people were not the only ones to invent the ball, which was known in ancient Egypt and Greece, but they did invent the all-important rubber ball, which makes so many of our present games possible. The Indians were also not the only ones to compete in teams on courts; we know that such games were played in the Eastern Hemisphere also. But ball playing and many other sports and athletics were an important part of Indian life, especially in Central and North America. This fact has been a great influence on sports of today. Nearly four hundred ancient stone-laid ball courts of various shapes and design have been found from Arizona southward through Mexico to Central America and the West Indies. There may once have been many more. One kind of court in Mexico had a stone ring set vertically on each of two side walls. The aim of the player was to pass the ball through one of the rings. Cortes and other explorers saw Aztec teams play this game. A description of the court reminds some people of our game of basket-

Competing teams of Dakota Indians are shown playing lacrosse in thi. watercolor titled *Ball Play, Traverse des Sioux* by Frank B. Mayer Lacrosse was popular with Indian people living in northern Nortl America and was enjoyed by the fur traders and explorers as early a. the 1600s. This painting was done in 1851.

Courtesy Goucher College, Baltimore

ball, but no records have been found linking our game with that of the Aztecs.

One Indian game that the Europeans did take over, however, is lacrosse. The French in Canada began to enjoy watching Indian teams play this game in the 1600s. Explorers and others have left numerous accounts of the sport. In time, the Europeans decided to take up the game themselves. During the 1800s there were many matches between Indian and Canadian teams. The Montreal Lacrosse Club was established in 1856, and in the following decade the Canadian Parliament formally adopted lacrosse as the national game of Canada. Demonstration matches were held in England and France during the 1860s between Iroquois and Canadian teams. One match was played before Queen Victoria at Windsor Castle. Such events may have encouraged the spread of the game throughout the British Isles. The English LaCrosse Union was founded in 1892. By that time the game had been somewhat changed from the sport

as played by the Indian teams. A code of rules had been established, and the original leather-covered hair ball had been replaced by one of sponge rubber. Lacrosse has long been popular in the United States among colleges, and clubs were organized as early as the 1870s. In the 1970s box lacrosse, a variation of the game, was added to professional sports in the United States.

It would be hard to imagine the United States, as well as many other nations today, without the organized sports that so heavily depend on the rubber ball and other elements from the Indian way of life. It is fitting that some teams should be called Chiefs, Braves, Warriors, Black Hawks—and Indians.

A number of Indian athletes have contributed to sports in today's world, and some have achieved high honor. James F. Thorpe, Sauk-Fox, all-around athlete, won medals at the Olympic Games in Stockholm in 1912. He was a member of the New York Giants for seven years, played professional football, and was one of the founders of the National Football League. Billy Mills, Oglala Sioux, won the first-place gold medal in the 10,000-meter race in the 1964 Olympic Games in Tokyo. The following year he made the second fastest three-mile run ever registered. Allie Reynolds, Creek, in baseball during the 1940s and 1950s, played with the Cleveland Indians and the New York Yankees. He was an American League All-Star for seven years. Joe Thornton, Cherokee, won the Olympic Medal as champion archer in Oslo, 1961. Charles A. Bender, Ojibwa, a major-league baseball player with the Philadelphia Athletics, was later a coach for the U. S. Naval Academy and the Chicago White Sox. Don Eagle, Mohawk, was a professional wrestler who also starred in football, track, lacrosse, and boxing.

Indian Words and Place Names

WHEN THE English colonists began writing letters back to England in the early 1600s, they used some words that the people there had never heard before—words like *squash, moccasin,* and *hominy,* spelled as they sounded to English ears. These may have been the first American Indian words to be taken into the English language. When the early Europeans learned to know and use an Indian object, the natural thing to do was to adopt the American expression for it. They began using the word *moccasin* when they learned to wear the Indian shoes with snowshoes and discovered that the Indian moccasins were more comfortable on the forest trails than their own hard-soled boots. They spoke of squash and hominy when they learned to eat those Indian foods. When they saw such strange animals as the chipmunk, opossum, skunk, and raccoon, what better than to call them by their Indian names? Nearly two hundred Indian words were taken into English from Algonquin, the speech of the people who lived in eastern Canada and the northeastern quarter of the United States. Among the words still in common use are *totem, hickory, moose, raccoon, caucus,* and *tamarack.* Another hundred were added from other Indian languages spoken north of Mexico.

Some Indian words came into English through the French and Spanish. From the French of eastern Canada, the colonists picked up such words as *caribou, toboggan,* and *mackinaw.* As the waves of white exploration and settlement rolled westward, Indian words came into English from the Spanish settlements in the Southwest. In addition, nearly two hundred words entered English through the Spanish from Indian tongues of Mexico, Central and South America, and the West Indies. Not long after they landed, Columbus and his men learned the words *maize, tobacco, hammock,* and *canoe,* or the native words from which they are derived. *Maize* and *canoe* were used in print as early as 1555. Other words that came from regions south of the border are *chocolate, chili, tomato, barbecue, pecan,* and *coyote.* Still others are *alpaca, llama, vicuña, cannibal, hurricane, potato,* and *avocado.* George Washington used the word *avocado* in his diary in 1751. In most cases, our present words are somewhat changed from the way they were first written down. In all, more than five hundred American Indian words were taken into English; many are still in use.

An expression we hear every day is *OK.* U.S. soldiers during World War II heard it almost everywhere they went. Although some scholars are not sure of its origin, Webster's dictionary says that the expression probably comes from the Choctaw language. The Choctaw Indians used the word *okeh* in their councils to show agreement. It meant "Yes, it is" or "We have reached a point where agreement is possible." That Indian word has come a long way.

Dozens of Indian words are still used in the French spoken in Canada. Thousands entered the languages of Spain and Portugal when men from those countries invaded Mexico and Central and South America. It is easy to understand why this should be, if we remember that the Europeans in those Indian lands lived among the people and enslaved them. The Native Americans who worked for the foreigners in the mines and fields knew only their own tongues, and the Euro-

These moccasins of black buckskin are embroidered with fine hair from moose hide, dyed in bright colors, and with designs of porcupine quill work. They were made by a Huron woman in Quebec 150 years ago.

pean overlords had to learn Indian words in order to talk to them. So many new words were taken into Spanish in the Americas—most of them from Indian languages, a few from other sources—that they fill a three-volume dictionary.

Some Indian words are also found today in other world languages. Most are in the languages of Europe, but a good many others have gone around the world. Usually the Indian word has followed the Indian product. The Indian word *tobacco,* for example, in slightly different forms, is found in many languages, including German, Dutch, Norwegian, Swedish, and Russian. The word *chocolate,* in some form, has also been taken into those languages, as well as into Persian, Japanese, Chinese, and other tongues. *Moccasin, tomato, toboggan,* and *canoe* have entered many world languages. Indeed Native American words are found almost everywhere on earth.

Some Indian words and phrases have entered English as translations, in such expressions as *paleface, bury the hatchet, warpath,* and *father of waters.* Many common English phrases are formed by adding the word *Indian* to other words, such as Indian summer, Indian meal, Indian club. Nearly a hundred such phrases can be found in Webster's dictionary.

The greatest number of Indian words adopted by the European invaders are names of places. In the United States, twenty-six states have Indian names: Alabama, Alaska, Arkansas, Arizona, Connecticut, Idaho, Illinois, Iowa, Kansas, Kentucky, Massachusetts, Michigan, Minnesota, Mississippi, Missouri, Nebraska, New Mexico, North Dakota, Ohio, Oklahoma, South Dakota, Tennessee, Texas, Utah, Wisconsin, Wyoming. Many of the nation's biggest cities have Indian names; they include Chicago, Kansas City, Miami, Milwaukee, Omaha, and Seattle. Other cities and smaller communities with Indian names are Kalispell, Keokuk, Mankato, Natchez, Peoria, Pocatello, Tacoma, Topeka, Tucson, Tulsa, and Wichita. In some cases, the present city stands where an Indian community of the same name once stood. Many studies have been made of local areas, to count the number of places with Indian names. One such study found five thousand in New England alone. Some Indian place names have been translated into English: Bad Axe, Battle Creek, Broken Bow, Medicine Hat, Moose Jaw, Red Wing. Others were translated into French: Baton Rouge, Coeur d'Alene, Des Moines, Eau Claire, Fond du Lac, and Mille Lacs. Streets in America's cities and villages add thousands more Indian names. The four dozen Indian street names in St. Paul, Minnesota, include Kasota, Mendota, Mesabi, Mohawk, Osage, Osceola, Owasso, Tuscarora, Wabasha, Wacouta, Waukon, Wayzata, Winona.

Thousands of North American lakes, rivers, creeks, and other waterways bear the names that the Indian people gave them. All the Great Lakes except Lake Superior have Indian names. Nearly all the principal rivers and hundreds of smaller streams in the United States have the names by which they were called long ago. Some of them are Illinois, Iowa, Minnesota, Mississippi, Missouri, Ohio, Potomac, Susquehanna, Wabash, Washita, Wisconsin.

Canadian provinces with Indian names are Manitoba, Ontario, Quebec, and Saskatchewan. Canadian cities are Ottawa, Saskatoon, Toronto, and Winnipeg. Hundreds of smaller communities in Canada also bear names that came from the American Indians. An even greater number of Indian place names can be found in Latin American nations.

Indian names are also used in other ways. You can shop at Apache Plaza, stay at an Algonquin Motel, picnic in a Cherokee Park, patronize a Sioux Trail Beauty Salon, or use the ervices of a Chippewa Motor Freight Corporation. We have Pontiac cars, panama hats, lima beans, pima cotton, Catawba grapes, and wyandotte chickens.

Several American poets have written about Indian names, but the truest and saddest words on the subject were spoken by the Indian leader Khe-tha-a-hi, or Eagle Wing. He saw the names as signs from the past, sad reminders of his people, who held the land sacred as the burial place of their ancestors—the land that was taken from them by foreign intruders: "My brothers, the Indians must always be remembered in this land. Out of our language we have given names to many beautiful things which will always speak of us. Minnehaha will laugh for us, Seneca will shine in our image, Mississippi will murmur our woes. The broad Iowa and the rolling Dakota and the fertile Michigan will whisper our names to the sun that kisses them. The roaring Niagara, the sighing Illinois, the singing Delaware, will chant unceasingly our Death Song. Can it be that you and your children will hear that eternal song without a stricken heart? We have been guilty of only one sin—we had possession of what the white man coveted. We moved away toward the setting sun; we gave up our homes to the white man."

CHAPTER

15

The Heritage of Indian Arts

THE ARTS of the Indian people have taken many forms. There are the architectural remains of ancient stone temples, pyramids, cliff dwellings, and other structures. There are other visual arts, such as sculpture, carvings, and painting. There are the crafts—here included in the arts—of weaving, beadwork, embroidery with dyed porcupine quills, and pottery and basket making. In other arts, the American Indians have produced and are still creating gifts of acting, music, and dance and many kinds of literature: poetry, legends and stories, writings on history, philosophy, religion, and other subjects.

Among the many kinds of art produced in South America in earlier times, the most important to have survived are examples of weaving and pottery, objects made of precious metals and copper, stone carvings, and many architectual remains.

From the Inca weavers have come textiles made from the cotton they raised and from the wool of the llama, alpaca, and vicuña—fabrics that are almost perfect in workmanship. Weaving that is more remarkable has survived from Peruvian civilizations that existed before the Incas, from delicate gauzes to rich multicolored tapestries. The most marvelous are the shawls, robes, ponchos, and mantles discovered in underground burial chambers on the Paracas peninsula and judged to be 1,500 to 2,500 years old. Everything about them

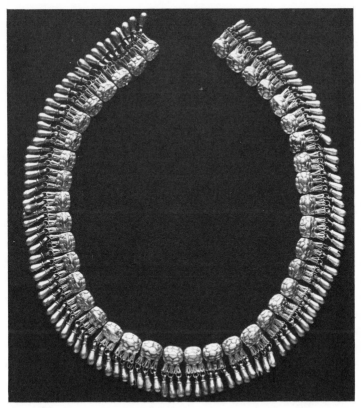

The goldsmith's art is illustrated in this exquisite necklace composed of forty turtle-shell-shaped beads from each of which hang three tiny gold bells, each with a gold clapper. It is the work of an artist of the Mixtec nation, who lived in western Mexico between 1300 and 1500.

is unusual: the fineness of the weaves, the softness of the wool, the richness and harmony of the colors, the originality of the weaving patterns and the embroidery. Even the size of the pieces—some being 13 feet wide and 84 feet long—is unusual. Many artists and scholars consider the Paracas textiles the most beautiful ever created.

Of the various kinds of pottery made in ancient South America, the finest is the thin-walled, delicate ware from Peru. Some pieces, with graceful shapes and bright-colored decorations, compare favorably with vases of Classical

Greece, considered the world's finest. Elegant painted and carved pottery has survived from ancient Ecuador and Brazil, also.

Metalwork was important to the people of Peru, Colombia, and Ecuador. They used copper to make ax blades, knives, and other tools, fashioning some so skillfully that the objects are works of art. Sometimes the craftsmen combined copper with tin to form bronze. The remarkable gold and silver artistry of the Incas is known to us chiefly through accounts left by the European conquerors. Although the Spanish invaders were awed by the beauty of the gold and silver jewelry, statues, and other objects, they nevertheless seized all they could find, melted them down, and shipped the precious metal to Spain to be made into coins. In Peru the only pieces that escaped were those that were buried in tombs. Many gold objects, however, have survived from ancient Colombia and Ecuador. The goldsmiths of those regions understood gold casting, soldering, hammering, and every other important method of handling the metal. The world's largest collection of gold articles is in the Gold Museum in Colombia, which has more than twenty thousand exquisitely worked pieces.

Stone carvings—some massive and powerful, some small and delicate—are also part of the artistic heritage of South America. Slabs carved to represent figures of warriors, found in Ecuador, may have been made as grave markers. Carved stone seats, from the same region, were probably used as ceremonial thrones. From Peru have come graceful stone bowls, tiny statuettes of animals, carved stone charms, even tiny beads of highly polished stone.

The textiles, pottery, sculpture, and metal objects of ancient South America may be seen in museums of Europe and the Americas, but for the architectural remains art lovers must travel to Peru and other western countries of the continent. There, along a 3,000-mile stretch on the Pacific coast, may be seen the remains of Inca cities destroyed by the

Spanish conqueror Francisco Pizarro and his men in the early 1500s, as well as countless ruins left by earlier civilizations. In the last 150 years archaeologists have cleared many ancient streets of jungle growth and restored the structures, revealing the superb architectural style and advanced city planning of the earlier ages. The Incas as well as several nations that preceded them were master builders with stone. Using no mortar, they built with giant blocks of granite, fitting them together with a care and precision that have never been equaled. In spite of the passage of time and the jolts of countless earthquakes, many of the massive walls stand as straight and solid today as when they were built.

When the Indian nations of South America were invaded and conquered by the Spanish and Portuguese, the people's way of life was shattered. Their arts, mainly lost, never recovered their former importance.

In South America today, however, some art is being produced that is purely Indian. Fine crafts are practiced that have strong Indian designs, colors, and other characteristics. In Colombia and Venezuela, craftsmen are weaving textiles that are chiefly Indian, although they show some European and other foreign influences. In Ecuador, weaving and other crafts of a high order are being practiced by Indian people. Fine Indian weaving is done today in Chile, Peru, and Bolivia. Basket making is a well developed craft in several northern countries of South America. These products are being bought by museums in Europe and the Americas.

Traveling north in our survey of the visual arts, we come to Central America and Mexico, the two regions to which archaeologists have given the name Middle America. Art objects from ancient times that have survived there are stone sculpture and carving, clay figures, pottery, and articles made by goldsmiths. The architectural remains of Middle America are the finest in the Western Hemisphere.

The Indian people of Middle America used stone not only for buildings but also for powerful sculptures. The strangest

The Aztec Calendar Stone, 12 feet across and weighing 24 tons, was found in 1790 by workmen digging a foundation in Mexico City. It shows the face of the Sun God in the center, surrounded by the names of days and various symbols relating to the worship of the sun. Two great fire serpents form the outer rim. The stone was carved between 1479 and 1481.

sculptures are giant stone heads six or seven feet high and weighing many tons each, a number of which were found in jungles of southern Mexico. Sculptors in several nations carved tall stone slabs, some as much as 35 feet tall, representing priests or rulers wearing ceremonial garments. The most famous piece of Mexican stone sculpture is the Aztec Calendar Stone. This huge disk, 12 feet high and weighing 24 tons, has the face of the Sun God in the middle, encircled by the names of days and by bands of symbols relating to the worship of the sun.

Beautiful art treasures remaining from early Middle America are vases, statues, pendants, and ornaments carved of semiprecious stone such as onyx and turquoise. The Maya artists left rare ornaments and small figures carved of jade.

Small whistles, figurines, and other objects modeled of clay were created by the people of several ancient Middle American nations. Thousands of tiny clay figures show men, women, and children from many stations in life engaged in various activities. Included in this art form are the many small wheeled objects, mentioned earlier, which prove that these people did invent the wheel, although they never used it for transportation, so far as we know.

Pottery was one of the most common crafts of early Middle America. Probably every family made its own ware for daily use. The best pottery of the region is thin, delicate, and very hard, almost like fine china. Some pieces are painted with bright-colored designs. Some are decorated with scenes of ceremonies, festivals, and other important events, reminding one of the Grecian urn of which the English poet John Keats sang so eloquently. Today these Indian works are valued in museums around the world.

The most exquisite art objects made in ancient Mexico were the ornaments created by the goldsmiths and silversmiths of the Mixtecs, a people conquered by the Aztecs. Like the other Spaniards in Peru, Cortes and his soldiers collected gold and silver objects in Mexico and sent them to Spain, where they were melted down for coins. A few examples of the works, however, remain. One article that Cortes sent to the Spanish monarch escaped destruction, perhaps because there was little gold on it. That is the glistening green-feather headdress of the Aztec emperor Montezuma, made from the plumes of the sacred bird, the quetzal. Today it is the prized possession of the Völkerkunde Museum in Vienna, Austria.

Modern historians and archaeologists long believed that some reports about the splendor of Mexican gold artistry were the boasting of conquistadores, but in 1931 the con-

Thirty miles from Mexico City are the partially restored ruins of the great ceremonial center of Teotihuacán. The outstanding structure in the ancient site is the magnificent pyramid, the Temple of the Sun, shown here, built by the Toltec people about A.D. 100.

Courtesy Library of Congress

tents of a tomb discovered in the ruins of Monte Alban, south of Mexico City, changed their minds. In the tomb archaeologists found a dazzling treasure of art objects. Besides heaps of pearls, they found *gold* rings, bracelets, beads, necklaces, and masks, all showing the superb workmanship and faultless artistic taste characteristic of the Mixtec artists. These rare objects are now on display in a museum built for them at Monte Alban.

Architectural remains of ancient cities and ceremonial centers are found throughout Mexico and upper Central America. As in South America, some have been uncovered and at least partially restored. In Central Mexico the most

outstanding ruins are those of the giant pyramids near Mexico City, the Temple of the Sun and the Temple of the Moon, standing amid the remains of Teotihuacán, a vast ceremonial center. Monte Alban, one of the most impressive city ruins in Mexico, is an example of the advanced city planning done by Indian engineers of ancient times.

The builders in Middle America used stone for their cities, as the Incas did, but their architecture is very different from that in South America. Most stone walls built by the Incas are smooth and polished, while many of those to the north are deeply carved with figures, symbols, designs, and in some places a form of picture writing. The buildings of the Mayas in southern Mexico and upper Central America are especially rich in these decorations, sometimes making the whole building a giant sculpture. Inside, the walls of some buildings are covered with paintings. Much, if not all, this architecture was painted, like that of ancient Greece.

In the jungle lowlands of Yucatán, Mexico, are these partially restored ruins of the Great Plaza in the Maya temple-city of Tikal, built about A.D. 400. The large structure in the background is a temple.

As in South America, when the Spanish forced their way of life on the people of Central America and Mexico, the native arts were almost destroyed. But strange to say, some conquerors had an interest in the history of the land and the people of Mexico. They began to preserve native art objects as early as the 1500s. This interest continued in the centuries that followed. Serious collecting began in the late 1700s when several important artifacts were found, among them the famous Calendar Stone of the Aztecs. These pieces were preserved, and the search for others continued. Eventually the government gave support to those who were collecting and preserving art objects from the nation's past. In the

1880s a museum was established to house the collections, which grew as explorations and excavations continued.

In 1964 the National Museum of Anthropology was built in Mexico City to house objects of many past cultures of Mexico and Central America. There and in other museums in Mexico, the great Indian art works of that nation may now be seen.

Today Mexico is the inheritor of two cultures and two peoples, the Indian and the European. The combination of the two produced a new culture, a new art, a new race. The race, called the mestizo, came into being because most of the first Spanish soldiers and government administrators in Mexico did not bring wives to America, and the Indians and Europeans began to intermarry almost at once. Today 80 percent of the people of Mexico are members of the mestizo race; 17 percent call themselves Indian; the rest are from Asia, Africa, Europe, and other parts of the world. The rich, colorful mestizo art of Mexico today can be seen in the giant murals that decorate the walls of public buildings, the paintings and sculpture, music and dance, poetry, and other art forms.

Some art being produced in Mexico today, however, may be called truly Indian. Finely made baskets, belts, and carrying cases woven in attractive patterns, and vivid cotton and woolen textiles are made in northern Mexico. Wood carving, unusual cloth appliqué, interesting beadwork, and weaving are coming from Panama. The best Indian art created in Central America at present is the rich variety of colorful weaving that is done in the highland villages of Guatemala. Besides being sold in shops throughout the world, this high quality cloth is bought and displayed in museums of Europe and the Americas.

In the United States and Canada, the coming of the Europeans resulted in a different situation from that in Middle and South America. North of the Mexican border, the European intruders and the Indian people generally did not live together or intermarry. The settlers in the East pushed the Indian people ever farther westward, taking their homelands and living separate from them. This resulted in "islands" of Indian culture, surrounded by the foreign society of the whites, with little mingling of the two races.

Traveling north from Mexico, we come first to the states of the Southwest. In this region, rich in various forms of Indian art, we find remains of many ancient cliff houses, complex stone structures with hundreds of rooms, built into the faces of cliffs. There also are large community houses made of stone and adobe, which the Spaniards called pueblos. The descendants of the first people who lived there, now also called Pueblos, still live in some of these remarkable structures. Many similar buildings are in ruins but are preserved as examples of the ancient architecture.

The Pueblo Indians, an agricultural people, were weaving native cotton in the Southwest thousands of years ago. Nomadic Navajos who migrated from the north about A.D. 1000 learned this craft from the Pueblos and eventually outdid their teachers. At first they wove only cotton. After the Spaniards brought in sheep the Navajos began to use wool, but the colors and designs of their art remained unchanged. The Navajos have continued to make woolen textiles. Their rugs and blankets, which are for sale in many countries, are widely known and admired. The Pueblos also taught the Navajos how to create sacred sand paintings, which are part of religious healing ceremonies. In this unique art form, designs are made by sprinkling sand and finely ground rock of various colors on a neutral background. The Navajos developed sand painting into an art of which they are today the recognized masters.

Kachina masks and dolls made by Pueblo artists are another well-known Indian art form of the region. The dolls, carved of wood, are brightly decorated with colored feathers, paint, and sometimes cloth. Although they were origi-

The most famous pottery made in the Southwest at present is the
black ware that was developed by Julian and Maria Martinez,
San Ildefonso Pueblo. The example shown here is from the private
collection of Dr. and Mrs. Frederick J. Dockstader.

Courtesy Museum of the American Indian, Heye Foundation

nally made to be used in religious ceremonies, both masks
and dolls are now also made to be sold to tourists.

Various kinds of excellent pottery were made in the southwestern states in ancient times, many pieces of which remain.
In modern times outstanding pottery is still being made
there. The most creative artists in the region have been
Julian and Maria Martinez, San Ildefonso Pueblo, whose
distinctive black ware is world renowned. Lucy Lewis and
Marie Chino, both Acoma Pueblo women, are known for
their black and white pottery. Nampeyo in Hopi ware; Mar-
garet Tafoya, Santa Clara Pueblo artist; and Rose Gonzales,

San Ildefonso Pueblo, with their red ware, have also contributed to the tradition of fine quality ware in the Southwest.

Navajo men learned metalwork from Mexican ironsmiths and leather workers in the 1850s, then applied their skill to the making of silver jewelry. Later they learned to add turquoise settings, creating the silver work so well known today. Zuni and Hopi smiths produced silver work of a slightly different style.

Weaving and basketry are the oldest crafts in the Southwest. The baskets, woven of grass, reeds, willow fiber, and other native plant materials, were once made by all people of the region. Today the Hopi, Pima, and Papago are almost the only ones who continue this ancient craft.

In the area that is now California, Indian people of past centuries developed a skill in weaving baskets that has never been surpassed. Their products—formed of reeds, finely split roots, and other plant fibers—were often interwoven with beads and feathers. Not many artists today know and practice the technique. Those museums are lucky which have some of the few remaining examples of the earlier works.

Traveling to northwestern North America, we come to the Pacific coastal area that was early settled by Native American salmon fishermen. North of Mexico, that region is surpassed only by the Southwest in the production of art. Indians of the Northwest, especially the Tlingits, are known for their fine blankets woven of shredded cedar bark and the hair of mountain goats, and baskets of cedar bark and spruce roots, woven so fine that they can hold water. More important, the Indian people there proved to be the most skillful woodworkers of North America. Living in a land of dense spruce and cedar forests, they used wood to make boats, cradles, dishes, masks, weapons, and many other articles. They used it, above all, for their totem poles. Each of these giant columns was carved with figures of birds, animals, and mythological creatures believed to be the ancestors of the

Navajo Weavers by Harrison Begay, well-known Navajo artist, portrays one woman spinning wool, the other weaving the kind of textile for which their people are world famous. In the left foreground is a basket of carded wool, ready to be spun. At the right is a basket holding balls of yarn.

Courtesy Philbrook Art Center, Tulsa, Oklahoma

person for whom the totem was made. Its purpose was to proclaim his wealth, accomplishments, and social standing.

Wood sculpture flourished among the Indian people of the Northwest long before the Europeans appeared. But when the white traders brought them steel tools, their art blossomed. The most productive period was from 1850 to 1900. The wood carving arts of the Indian people of the Northwest have changed with the times, but even now fine artists in the area are working in the style of their ancestors.

The Indians of the Plains, principally the Dakota or Sioux, became the most widely known of the Native Americans probably because they appeared in Wild West shows during the last century and in western movies of more recent times. Many people today, especially Europeans, still think that all Indians of earlier times were buffalo-hunting horsemen. The Plains people created the dramatic costume that is still generally, though mistakenly, looked on as the typical American Indian dress: the fringed buckskin shirt, decorated leggings, brightly beaded moccasins, and eagle-feather war bonnet. Since the Plains people lived off the buffalo, the hide of this animal was their major resource. They made it into clothing, tepee covers, carrying cases, shields, and other objects. In early times the Indians decorated the hides with embroidery, using dyed porcupine quills—a unique craft. Later the same designs were made using colored beads bought from the white traders. Buffalo hides were painted with scenes of events in the life of the people or of the painter. When hides became scarce, Indian artists substituted muslin or even paper obtained from the traders for their paintings. Fortunately some fine examples of all these Plains arts have survived. Many of the best, collected during the 1800s by European travelers, are now in collections in Germany, France, England, and other countries of Europe. Bead and quill embroidery and the making of costumes—out of buckskin and other materials—is still carried on by Plains Indian craftsmen today.

This shoulder bag, beautifully embroidered with bead designs, was made by a Shawnee artist about 1825.

Courtesy Museum of the American Indian, Heye Foundation

In the Central Woodlands, the Indian people used materials from the forest to make things they needed. The bark of the birch tree had the most uses. It could be fashioned into many articles, the most important of which was the slender, graceful canoe. Like the people of the Northwest, the central woodland dwellers were skilled wood carvers, but few of the articles they created in past centuries have survived. The Ojibwa were especially known for their ornate carrying cases or bandolier bags. First made of deerskin and decorated with quill embroidery, the bags were later made of trade cloth and embellished with glass beads in vivid patterns of flowers and leaves.

The Iroquois, original dwellers in the northeastern woodlands, were and still are skilled in several arts and crafts. As wood-carvers they have long been known for their false-face masks. They also made baskets of grasses, reeds, cornhusks, and wood splints. The Algonquin people of eastern Canada had similar art styles and were especially skilled at working with birchbark. Today baskets, floral beadwork, masks, and quill embroidery are still being made by the Indian people of the Northeast.

Indians along both the Atlantic and Pacific coasts made wampum—shell beads that were formed into strings or woven into belts. Certain kinds were used as money. Other kinds were made to decorate clothing. Wampum belts woven with figures and designs to convey messages served as official documents to bind agreements between nations or as sacred objects in religious rites. They were important in the government operations of the Iroquois, who made some of the finest wampum.

One advanced Indian culture north of Mexico was located in the southeastern United States. Some of the richest art of ancient America was created in that area. The works that have survived are examples of delicate, polished pottery, clay figures, and statues and pipes carved of stone. Although the old culture ended long ago, some mountain and forest dwellers of the Southeast today are creating fine stone carvings and weaving baskets, using many designs, colors, and methods of their ancestors.

Long ago every Indian man and woman had to be skilled in making articles for everyday use. Today most Indian people have become part of the "American" way of life: they work as teachers, clerks, sales persons, farmers, lawyers, truck drivers, like the rest of the population. But many are artists and craftsmen, too, as we have seen. Dozens of American Indian painters in various parts of the United States are doing outstanding work. Harrison Begay, probably the most widely known Navajo painter, is internationally recognized. Pablita Velarde, Santa Clara Pueblo, is well known as a painter of Pueblo daily life. The works of Fred Kabotie, often referred to as the dean of Pueblo Indian painters, portray Hopi legends and ceremonies. Oscar Howe, a gifted Sioux artist, follows the painting traditions of his people. Carl Gowboy and Patrick Desjarlait, Ojibwa painters, present Indian themes in their works. Ojibwa artist George Morrison, professor of art at the University of Minnesota, has won fame for his work in both Europe and America. Charles Huntington, also Ojibwa, is a nationally known creator of metal sculpture. Dozens more could be named, including those in Latin America.

Besides producing their own art, the Indian people have provided subjects for many distinguished non-Indian painters. Most of these artists lived among the Native American people before their way of life had been seriously corrupted by white influence. One was George Catlin, who traveled through the West and learned to respect and appreciate the Indian culture. Others whose art was inspired by the Indian people are Seth Eastman, Paul Kane, Peter Rindisbacher, and John Mix Stanley. A number of distinguished artists came from Europe to paint American Indian scenes, and many of their works are now in European galleries. Native American influence can also be seen in some present-day architecture, especially in the Southwest. One example is the New Mexico statehouse.

In acting, music, and the dance, less remains from the past, for these arts could leave no records, but much is being produced by Indian people in the present.

Among Indian actors and entertainers, Will Rogers, a popular Cherokee humorist of the first part of the 1900s, is one of the best known. His comments on the human race, as true

Scimitar, a 23-foot brass figure, is the work of Charles Huntington, nationally known sculptor who lives in Minneapolis, Minnesota. It was commissioned in 1974.

Courtesy, General Mills, Inc., Minneapolis

today as they were fifty years ago, are still printed in daily newspapers. Chief Dan George, of the Squamish people, won the 1970 New York Film Critics' Award as best supporting actor for his role as Old Lodge Skins in the film *Little Big Man*. Jay Silverheels, a Mohawk, was known to those who enjoy western movies for his part as Tonto in *The Lone Ranger*. Will Sampson, a member of the Creek tribe, was a success in the film *One Flew Over the Cuckoo's Nest* and was quickly signed to play in several westerns. Buffy Sainte-Marie, of the Cree tribe, is a well-known Indian musician who composes and sings her own songs. The Cherokee actress and singer Keely Smith has won many awards for her performances.

Louis Ballard, a Quapaw-Cherokee man, is one of the few American Indian composers who write for non-Indian musicians today. His compositions, which recall ancient themes and rhythms, introduce an exciting element into non-Indian music. Some of his works use native musical instruments along with the more traditional. One choral work includes a tribal song. Ballard's American Indian ballets have been successfully performed by Indian dancers.

Non-Indian composers have used Indian material for nearly two centuries, although it is hard to recognize Indian sources in their music. Edward MacDowell's *Indian Suite* and several works by Charles Skilton are considered the best works showing such influence. Some music historians believe that the special rhythm that is vital to jazz can be traced to Indian music: the steady beat of the drum accompanied by singing in a different beat.

A number of Indian men and women have become outstanding performers in ballet and modern dance. Among the most famous are Maria and Marjorie Tallchief of the Osage tribe. Maria Tallchief, one of the world's great ballerinas, was the star of the New York City Ballet Company. Her sister starred in the Paris Opera Ballet. Donald Saddler, who has an Indian heritage, is a world renowned dancer and choreographer (composer or designer of dances). José Limón, who had Indian ancestors, organized and headed one of the great modern dance companies of the twentieth century. In addition, at least a dozen young Indian men and women are performing in important dance companies in the United States and Canada.

In the literary arts, the Indian people have been creative for many centuries. In South America, the highly cultured Incas had no written language, but kept their records by means of the quipus mentioned earlier, which have never been deciphered. Some Inca poetry and writings on history, religion, government, and other matters have, however, been preserved. After the conquest, some educated Spaniards in Peru began to write down works that the Incas dictated to them, works that had been transmitted orally. One important history was written by Garcilaso de la Vega—the son of a royal Inca woman and a Spanish knight—who set down what he had been told by his Inca ancestors.

In ancient Mexico, all the advanced cultures had forms of writing and produced large bodies of literature on a variety of subjects. The books of the Aztecs, Mixtecs, Mayas, and others, many of them illustrated with colored drawings, were highly valued by the people. Unfortunately the Spanish burned all the writings they could find—indeed whole librar-ies—in their zeal to destroy the "works of the devil." "We burned them all," wrote one priest, speaking of the Maya books, adding that the people "regretted this to an amazing degree, which caused them much suffering."

Five Maya books that somehow escaped destruction are now in museums in France, Spain, and Russia, treasured as works of art. So far as they can be deciphered, they deal with astronomy, religion, and the Maya calendar. Of the many books of the Mixtecs, Aztecs, and other Mexican and Central American people, fourteen remain. They also can be only partly read.

Does this mean that we know nothing of the literature of

the ancient Mexicans? Not at all. In fact we know a great deal about it. Most of the literature—even the written work —was also passed down by word of mouth. Their educated men knew the histories, sacred writings, laws, poetry, and legends by heart, just as the poets, storytellers, and tribal chroniclers of ancient Europe and Asia did. After the conquest, some of them learned Spanish and began to write down what had been in the books that the Spaniards burned. Others wrote in their own languages, using European script. As early as the mid-1500s some Spanish scholars, military men, and priests who had learned the native languages began to question the people about their history, songs, legends, and other matters and wrote down what was recited to them. In this way much literature of ancient Mexico was preserved.

In the regions north of Mexico, now the United States and Canada, Indian literature was rescued in the same way. Here the literature of the people was all in oral form. It consisted of an unbelievable amount and variety of songs, poems, legends, lives of heroes, philosophy, religious rituals, moral precepts, history, and tales explaining man's place in the universe. By the 1700s, some of the less prejudiced non-Indians began to realize that here was a treasure of thought that should be preserved in written form. Some historians, scientists, soldiers, even missionaries began to write down the things dictated to them by Indian people. In that way great numbers of books were written.

Indian people themselves, some of them scholars, also took part in this work. One of them was Sequoya (see KWOY a), a Cherokee, and an intellectual genius. He created an alphabet and devised rules for writing the language of his people. Through him, thousands of members of the tribe learned to read and write their native tongue. John N. B. Hewitt, a Tuscarora, and Francis La Flesche, of the Omaha nation, are authors of writings on early Indian history for the Smithsonian Institution. Ella Deloria, Sioux, a faculty member of Columbia University, was a historian and linguist. Arthur C.

Parker, a Seneca scholar, was archaeologist for the New York State Museum. There were many others. In some instances American Indians spoke through interpreters to writers who took down their thoughts. One of them was the famous Sioux holy man and philosopher Black Elk.

Thus from north to south in the hemisphere the ancient literature of the Indian people was gathered and written down, much as the tales of the ancient Greeks, Anglo-Saxons, and other ancient peoples were recorded centuries earlier. This great body of American literature—now numbering thousands of volumes—is being studied by scholars, many of them Indian, and gradually brought to the attention of the public. Few people realize the literary quality of many of these works. In fact this heritage of American thought is almost unknown except to writers and scholars.

Indian subjects have furnished inspiration for hundreds of non-Indian novelists, poets, and playwrights both in the Americas and in Europe. The most important early American novelist to deal with Indian subjects is James Fenimore Cooper. His *Leatherstocking Tales,* not always historically correct, were the first to win recognition for American literature in Europe. The most famous poem on an Indian subject is no doubt *The Song of Hiawatha* by Henry Wadsworth Longfellow. Admiring readers of the poem do not seem to mind that the story is a hopeless tangle of Indian history and myth. Karl May, a German writer of the late 1800s, wrote many novels about North American Indian life that were immensely popular and are still read. No matter how these works may be judged, they do show the influence that Indian cultures have had on the literature of the non-Indian world.

Meanwhile, Native American writers continue to produce literature. They no longer communicate through interpreters and scribes, but speak for themselves, in voices that are heard and respected. American Indian authors are writing books on many subjects, making contributions unlike any others. Frederick J. Dockstader, Oneida, long the director of the Museum of the American Indian, Heye Foundation, in New York, has written authoritatively on many aspects of Indian art. D'Arcy McNickle, Flathead-Kootenai, author of such historical works as *Indian Tribes of the United States* and novels—*The Surrounded* and *Runner in the Sun*—is one of the writers of the *Encyclopedia Britannica.* N. Scott Momaday, Kiowa, has written history and fiction. His novel *House Made of Dawn* won the Pulitzer Prize for fiction in 1969. Other well-known American Indian writers today are James Welch, Blackfoot, and Gerald Vizenor, Ojibwa. Beginning in the 1960s, the pride and dignity of the American Indians gave rise to a new kind of writing that is best illustrated by the works of Vine Deloria, Jr., a Sioux writer. His books, including *Custer Died for Your Sins, An Indian Manifesto,* and *God Is Red,* challenge the unjust judgments of history and express a growing demand that American Indians be given their rightful place in America's past and present.

CHAPTER
16
Rediscovering the Gift Givers

WE HAVE seen how the material and spiritual gifts of the American Indians have benefited and influenced humankind, how they were adopted by Europeans and eventually affected cultures in all parts of the world. Yet, strangely, hundreds of years passed before the Indian people were given any credit for these gifts. The story of how this happened is a mystery that has taken centuries to unravel, and it is still unfolding.

When the Spanish conquistadores invaded Mexico and South America in the early 1500s, they laid waste the principal cities, demolished temples, smashed sculpture, and burned books. Buildings which they did not destroy during the conquest they tore down later, using the stone to build churches, mansions, and government offices. They enslaved the defeated people, who sank into poverty and despair. In the first century of occupation, the Indian population was reduced to less than half by disease, hunger, war, and other disasters. Many abandoned their ruined cities and fled to the mountains, where they hoped to survive. As the years passed, dust and sand settled on the stone streets. Tangled jungle vines crept over the remains of towers, libraries, sunken gardens, and broad city squares that had once so amazed the Spanish conquerors. Gradually the great Indian civilizations of Mexico and Peru sank out of sight and were forgotten.

But all the while this was happening, another force was at work. Among the conquerors were some who saw the greatness of the Indian cultures and regretted their destruction. These men began, almost at once, to make records of what they saw. One of the best accounts was written by a talented young soldier who wrote thousands of pages of firsthand information about the people, their history, and their way of life. Another was written by a fellow soldier of Cortes who observed, remembered, and set down his experiences. Some Spanish priests studied the Indian languages, questioned the people, and wrote down what they learned. Other accounts were written by sons of Spanish soldiers and Inca women. Some records were illustrated with drawings, adding further to the information being preserved. Government officials wrote hundreds of reports, through the years, dealing with conditions in the Spanish colonies of the New World.

Most of these documents were sent to Spain, where they were laid away in the royal archives—the public records of the kingdom—in Madrid. As the years passed, mountains of manuscripts accumulated, filling an entire library. But very few of the writings were published; some may not even have been read. In fact, they were locked away by the authorities. Spain did not want other nations to know about the wealth in its colonies or about the cruel treatment of the Indian people there. No foreigners were allowed to enter the Spanish colonies in the New World. Thus, centuries passed—the 1500s and 1600s, and into the 1700s—while the rest of the world knew almost nothing of what was going on in Mexico and South America and even less of what had been there before the Europeans came.

The 1700s brought a stirring of new ideas in Europe, a birth of interest in scientific exploration and events of the distant past. It became fashionable to have a curiosity about things antique; European gentlemen made tours to faraway places to examine ancient ruins and wonders of nature. Mexico and South America were still closed to foreigners, but a change was coming. To gain favor in France the Spanish king, in 1735, allowed a French scientific expedition to enter South America—although the group was to be accompanied by two Spanish naval officers. In this expedition, mentioned earlier, foreigners were for the first time given such permission. Since their main purpose was to make measurements of the earth at the equator, they were "deemed harmless." The changed attitude of Spain was shown later in the century by a king who himself sponsored archaeological work in Mexico. Still later, when the ruins of some Maya cities were discovered in the 1770s that king sent word that they were to be carefully explored, artifacts preserved, and drawings made. The Aztec Calendar Stone and other large stone carvings, found before 1800, were preserved and made part of an official collection.

Among the many scientific explorers of the time, the greatest was the German naturalist-geographer Alexander von Humboldt. With a letter bearing the Spanish royal seal, he traveled "for the acquisition of knowledge," in South America and Mexico. Between 1799 and 1804 he covered nearly 40,000 miles, much of it on foot. He climbed mountains, explored rivers, studied plants and animals, measured altitudes, collected bales of specimens, drew maps, and made bulging bundles of notes. In Peru he inspected Inca ruins and made the first accurate drawings of Inca roads and buildings. In Mexico, where he spent eleven months, he examined Aztec ruins, made sketches, and wrote descriptions.

Before leaving Mexico, Humboldt accepted an invitation to visit President Thomas Jefferson. He spent eight weeks in the United States, three of them with Jefferson in Washington. Jefferson was one of the few men of his time who had an interest in Indian cultures, and he wanted to learn more about them.

Returning to Europe, Humboldt began to write about his five-year journey in the Americas. When his books were published, in the early 1800s, the world for the first time found out about the immense empires of the Mayas, Aztecs, and Incas. Humboldt's writings about the ancient buried and forgotten Indian cultures kindled the interest that led to the work of rescuing them.

Through the labors of other explorers and archaeologists in the years that followed, the world learned more and more about the great Indian cultures of earlier times. Additional ruins were found in jungles and deserts, on mountains and seashores. Tombs were discovered containing rare objects that had not seen the light of day for thousands of years.

But all this news resulted in a mystery. Who were the people who created the advanced civilizations that were revealed by the excavations in Mexico and South America? Who designed the cities, built the temples and pyramids, laid out the roads and vast aqueduct systems, and carved the stone sculptures? Few believed that the Indian people then living in the Spanish colonies could have produced them. Yet how did these cultures arise?

Strange theories were put forward in answer to this question. One of the most widely accepted was that the American kingdoms were created by ancient wandering Jews—a theory firmly believed by sober scholars. Other historians suggested that the civilizations were created by ancient Greeks, Romans, Phoenicians, and other peoples from the Eastern Hemisphere.

Nothing was known at that time of the origins of the early American civilizations, and few historians had any serious interest in the subject. One man who did not believe the fantastic tales was a Boston lawyer, William Prescott, who decided to make a thorough investigation of the history of the ancient Mexican and Peruvian kingdoms. He knew of the mountains of dusty, long-neglected manuscripts, written centuries before, locked in the Spanish archives—firsthand records of the early American cultures. Prescott could read and write Spanish well, and with the help of influential friends got royal permission to use the writings. He could not go to Spain himself (he was nearly blind), but he paid scholars and secretaries to select and copy all the manuscripts dealing with his subjects—more than 8,000 pages—and bring them to him in Boston. The results of Prescott's labors were two impressive volumes, *The Conquest of Mexico* and *The Conquest of Peru*, published in the mid-1800s. These writings proved beyond a doubt that the Native American peoples, the Indians, had indeed created the splendid Maya, Aztec, and Inca civilizations. Prescott dealt not only with the stone ruins and other material remains. He described the commerce and agriculture of the nations, explained their complex government administrations, wrote of their religions, customs, and accomplishments. In short, he painted a faithful picture of the life and character of the people, giving his readers an idea of the greatness of the ancient kingdoms.

Prescott's books led the Spanish government to examine the old documents in its possession and publish many of them. Spanish manuscripts of the 1500s and 1600s were also discovered in attics and storerooms in other countries of Europe. Some had been taken off Spanish ships by pirates, along with other loot, in earlier centuries. A few valuable writings were found and published as late as the 1920s. Thus more and more of the forgotten past was brought to light.

Meanwhile, the work of Humboldt and other scientists stimulated further searches and excavations. In Mexico and later in Peru, native-born archaeologists began to take an increasing part in rediscovering the past greatness of their countries. They are doing the chief work today. As time passed and more lost ruins were uncovered, scholars realized that other great civilizations existed long before the three kingdoms that were conquered in the 1500s. Even today, only a relatively few of the ruins in Mexico and Peru have been uncovered and restored; more are being found in jungles, deserts, and mountains. The work still goes on, most of it now under regulations of the local governments. Thousands of books have been written describing every aspect of life in the ancient Americas, and more are being produced.

Prescott "gave America back to the Indians," but by the mid-1800s the Indian people had still been given almost no credit for the many valuable American plants that the world had adopted and put to use. When these products were taken to Europe in the 1500s, herbalists there (the fathers of modern botany) tried to make each plant fit into the descriptions they found in the writings of the ancient Greeks and Romans. They simply took for granted that the plants had originated in the Eastern Hemisphere—all except tobacco and sunflowers. These, they decided, must be American.

Not until nearly four centuries after Columbus was this absurd mistake corrected. In the 1880s a French botanist, preparing to write a book on the origins of cultivated plants, examined the early records of the fruits, vegetables, and other produce that had come from the Americas. The longer he searched, the clearer it became to him that the plants which the European explorers and conquerors found in the Americas were all native to those continents. He began to see that many of them must have been domesticated from wild plants by Indian farmers and plant breeders in both North and South America. His book was the first written source of such information.

During the early 1900s the U.S. Department of Agriculture continued research on the subject. In the 1920s this resulted in a book, *The Beginnings of American Agriculture,* which gave still more credit to the American Indian people for the development of crops that have, through the centuries, proved to be so valuable. Later studies recognized the native genius of the early Indians in developing more than forty plants that have proved useful to the human race. It is estimated that the many food crops, as well as cotton, rubber, tobacco, quinine, and others, account for at least half of the world's agriculture.

In the regions now occupied by the United States and Canada, ancient Indian civilizations also existed, but they left no ruins of stone cities to uncover. Important cultures did, however, exist north of Mexico at the time the white men arrived, cultures that contributed to the riches and welfare of the Europeans. We saw how the explorers, traders, and colonists benefited from many kinds of help from the American Indians in the northern regions. Yet as the years passed, these benefits became covered over and hidden, not by jungle vines and blowing sand, but by forgetfulness and lack of acknowledgment. The many elements of Indian culture became so intertwined with the non-Indian way of life that their source was slowly lost. Gradually the white people forgot that the first colonists survived only with Indian help; that the corn, cotton, tobacco, peanuts, and other crops on which the nation had grown rich all came from the Indians.

In 1903, more than four centuries after Columbus, Alexander Chamberlain became the first scholar to survey the record of Indian gifts. In an article called "The Contributions of the American Indians to Civilization" he listed the many ways that the Native Americans added to the "health, happiness, wealth, and wisdom" of mankind. After him, other scholars began to look at the record of Indian accomplishments. Since the mid-1900s many American histories have included some mention of the part that the Indian people have played in world culture.

But the recognition of mankind's debt to the Indian is still far from complete. Few people realize that, in the United States especially, an enormous part of our life is Indian. We eat Indian foods every day, wear clothes made of Indian cotton, ride on tires made of Indian rubber along highways that follow Indian trails, smoke Indian tobacco, use Indian inventions, enjoy Indian arts and recreations, benefit from

Indian medicines, follow Indian democratic traditions, live in cities located on Indian village sites, in states with Indian names.

Indians are not figures of the past, who stood in the way of the white man's progress. They played a great part in making that progress possible. American Indians are an indestructible part of the past and a living part of the present. Their part in the future can be no less.

Bibliography

Brown, Francis J., ed. *Our Racial and National Minorities.* New York: Prentice-Hall, 1952.

Cohen, Felix. "Americanizing the White Man," *The American Scholar,* Vol. 21 (Spring 1953), pp. 177–191.

Dockstader, Frederick J. *Indian Art.* New York: Museum of the American Indian, 1973.

Hallowell, A. Irving. "The Impact of the American Indian on American Culture," *American Anthropologist* New Series, Vol. 59 (April 1957), pp. 201–221.

Harrington, John P. *Our State Names.* Washington: Smithsonian Institute, 1955.

Hetzel, Theodore B. "We Can Learn From American Indians," *Journal of American Education,* Vol. 4 (May 1965), pp. 23–26.

La Fay, Howard. "The Maya, Children of Time," *National Geographic,* Vol. 148 (December 1975), pp. 729–767.

McDowell, Bart. "Mexico's Window on the Past," *National Geographic,* Vol. 134 (October 1968), pp. 492–521.

McIntyre, Loren. "The Lost Empire of the Incas," *National Geographic,* Vol. 144 (December 1973) pp. 729–788.

Taylor, Norman. *Plant Drugs That Changed the World.* New York: Dodd, Mead & Co., 1965.

Vogel, Virgil J. *This Country Was Ours.* New York: Harper & Row, 1972.

Von Hagen, Victor W. *Ancient Sun Kingdoms of the Americas.* New York: World Publishing Co., 1957.

Index

Page numbers in italics refer to illustrations.

Cortes, 104; raised in Virginia colony, 39, 109, 110; adopted by Europeans, 107, 109; cigarettes, 110, 111, 112; use in U.S., 1900s, 110, 111, 112; opposition to use, 111–13; ill effects of use, 111–13; as protein, 113–15. *See also* Pipes, tobacco

Toboggan, Indian invention, 136

Tomatoes: use by Indian people, 62; adopted by Europeans, 62; and Jefferson, 62

Totem poles, 166–7

Trails, Indian: extent, 47–8; Iroquois Trail, 49–50, map, *49*; Nemacolin's Path, 50; Warrior's Path, 51–2; map, *51*; Big Medicine Trail, 52–3

U   V

Vanilla: produced by Indians, 63–4; process for making, 64; and Aztecs, 63, 64; adopted by Europeans, 64

Velarde, Pablita, 171

Vicuña: use by Incas, 122; adopted by Europeans, 122–3

Virginia, colony: saved by tobacco crop, 39, 109; aided by Indians, 38–9

Vizenor, Gerald, 177

W   X   Y   Z

Wampum, shell bead, 170

Warrior's Path, map, *51*

Weaving and weavers: Inca, 154; Paracas, 154–5; S. American, 157; Mexican, 163; Navajo, 164, *167*; Pueblo, 164; Northwest, 166, 170; Guatemala, 163; Southwest, 166

Welch, James, 177

Wheel, Indian invention, 130, *130*

Wilderness Road, former Indian trail, 51–2

Wilson, Peter, Iroquois leader, and conservation, 48–9

Zero, Maya invention, 129–30

About the Author

HERMINA POATGIETER, a Phi Beta Kappa graduate of the University of Iowa, was a member of the research and writing staff of the Minnesota Historical Society for more than twenty years. She was editor of the Society's magazine for young people and is co-author of *Outdoors: Adventures in Conservation.*